Ireland at the Crossroads

Ireland at the Crossroads

Lisdoonvarna, Direct Provision and the Far Right

Theresa O'Donohoe

ORPEN PRESS

Published by
Orpen Press
Upper Floor, Unit B3
Hume Centre
Hume Avenue
Park West Industrial Estate
Dublin 12

email: info@orpenpress.com
www.orpenpress.com

Paperback ISBN 978-1-78605-130-1
ePub ISBN 978-1-78605-131-8

Printed in Dublin by SPRINTprint Ltd

Contents

*This book is dedicated to my inspiring, witty and caring children.
I love you dearly and strive to leave this world a safer place for you.*

*Also, my parents. Tony, who taught me camogie, justice and not to
combine the two. In memory of my late mother, Susie, who was a
warrior in the battle for mental health services.*

1

Breaking News

Lisdoonvarna

Hailed as the gateway to the Burren, Lisdoonvarna is a small town in the north of County Clare, Ireland. It is close to Slieve Elva, with views across the green fields to the cliffs at Doolin, onto the wind-swept Aran Islands, over to the dark hills of Connemara in Galway and around to the vast limestone veneer. The Burren was carved out as the last ice age receded. It is a karst landscape of bedrock, incorporating a vast cracked pavement of glacial-era limestone, with stunning cliffs, wildflowers, caves, fossils, rock formations and archaeological sites.

In the town of Lisdoonvarna there are numerous wells with water containing different minerals, including sulphur, magnesium, iron, and copper. The wells were developed and baths were built in the nineteenth century, so it's a relatively new town built as a tourist centre. Most of the present guest houses and hotels were built to accommodate the huge increase in visitor numbers to the spa. There were twelve hotels at one point but only half that number are in use now.

We moved here during the summer of 2015 in the middle of the tourist season. There was great life about the place, with music in the bars and hotels every night. While there was work going on at my house I used to go to a local hotel cafe to escape the mess, have some lunch and connect to their Wi-Fi to check in on the outside world. I loved to sit by the window and soak up the holiday atmosphere as people leisurely strolled around.

I wasn't prepared for the massive change of pace in September. Lisdoonvarna is home to an annual matchmaking festival when singles from all over the world come in search of love. It's a tradition going back decades. The story goes that after the harvest, farmers would head to the baths, drink the mineral-rich waters, sing, dance and look for a wife. Things have changed through the years, as sun holidays have flooded the market and the baths have closed. However, drinking the waters and courting are still very much part of the custom. The weekdays are filled with music and dancing, while every weekend throughout September sees thousands of visitors to the area.

After all the fun and frolics of September I definitely wasn't prepared for the pace of October. I headed up to the cafe with my laptop and could not believe how quiet the town was. Without any warning the cafe was closed. That was how it remained for almost six months, until the tourist season kicked off again with the arrival of St Patrick's Day. Hibernation is very much a part of life in Lisdoonvarna.

The Community Reaction

I first heard about plans for asylum seekers to be moved to Lisdoonvarna on Tuesday 20 February 2018. A close friend messaged me to ask if I had heard that Syrian refugees were relocating to Lisdoonvarna. My response was to suggest we look into what we could do to welcome them. I innocently assumed it would be that simple, having witnessed Ennistymon welcome families from war-torn Syria. Our ideas must have been very different, because within one week our friendship was over. We went from meeting up regularly, walking, planning community events and messaging each other at least twice a day, to nothing. I had lost my best friend in Lisdoonvarna within a week.

The following day I got a taste of how people were taking the news. I was in town when a man I regularly met out and about stormed in looking very angry. He had heard about plans to convert a local hotel into a centre for international refugees. His voice was raised and he was absolutely furious that the owner of the hotel, who he knew well, would make these plans without discussing it with him first. I got the impression he had considered the hotel owner a friend.

Anger is understandable when contracts affecting your community are made without anyone in the community being involved. I had personal experience of a similar situation where we had lived previously, in County Laois. Two energy companies had planned to erect hundreds of industrial wind turbines in the Midlands to export electricity to the UK. The companies had come into communities and secretly signed non-disclosure contracts with landowners who had reportedly been identified by state agencies. This is how the Irish government facilitates private profiteering without consideration for communities or the environment. Anger is a natural reaction in these situations.

On Wednesday afternoon, I headed to Dublin and was away for the following few days, having fun showing school children how to be activists. I was part of a team at An Taisce's Green Schools expo. My hair looked like a rainbow unicorn and I was discussing environmental issues with young people. I was doing what I love to do, but living so rurally I rarely get the opportunity. While I was away it emerged that the official proposal was to open a Direct Provision centre in one of the hotels. This would provide asylum seekers with full board accommodation and various services while their applications for asylum are processed as per the International Protection Act of 2015 in Irish law.

I missed out on engaging with the physical community response but I was pretty well informed via social media. A lot of the conversation was around services and the ability of a village with such a small population to cater for an increase of 115 new residents. Lisdoonvarna began trending on Twitter but I didn't recognise anyone who was discussing it.

I read some pretty disgusting racist posts on Twitter and on Facebook. Those opposed for racist reasons were the most vocal, often attacking anyone who showed a hint of consideration for asylum seekers. Local businesses were regulars on Twitter and watched with concern as their #Lisdoonvarna became a focal point for racism, with #SaveLisdoonvarna used to claim our village was under some sort of attack. I also read posts arguing that we needed to do our bit for those seeking refuge.

The community of Lisdoonvarna was thrown into a state of what I can only describe as bewilderment. People were finding out information in bits and pieces, leaving them desperate for more information on what exactly was planned for the area. The Department of Justice and Equality's policy is to issue tenders for accommodation providers and not to disclose anything until the contract is almost, if not already, signed. There was no public information point or person for us to go to with queries. This information void created a vacuum for others to speculate in and provide our community with misinformation. A lot of misinformation was shared on social media. Government policy and practice left us wide open to this situation.

On Friday 23 February, while I was away, an official from the Reception and Integration Agency (RIA), came to Lisdoonvarna to explain the plans and answer the community's questions. He was joined by the hotel owner at a top table in the community hall. One of my friends attended this public meeting and reported that it was very heated, with a lot of raised voices and some shouting. People were obviously angry. Some of the attendees voiced strong racist opinions, and they were the most vocal. They shared stories about riots and violence in Germany and asserted that if something similar happened here it would destroy Lisdoonvarna. Someone stated that the value of their house would drop. They were convinced that housing asylum seekers would damage the area and were not afraid to say so, very loudly.

The Cambridge Dictionary defines racism as:

> the belief that people's qualities are influenced by their race and that the members of other races are not as good as the members of your own, or the resulting unfair treatment of members of other races.

My friend attended the meeting with the intention of supporting the proposal to house asylum seekers in our community. In the end she said nothing but asked me to accompany her to the next meeting for moral support. I was reluctant to attend for a couple of reasons. I was a relatively new resident and thought this might be best left to the well-established locals. I had also decided I needed a break from voluntary work for a while. Having led the Tidy Towns initiative the previous year, my New Year's resolution had been to take a burnout break.

On Sunday 25 February, a Facebook page called 'Direct Provision Lisdoonvarna Group' was created that provided diplomatic insight into the initial thinking. The page had the following information and description:

> Late on Tuesday evening 20 February 2018 word leaked to the community that the owner of four major hotels in Lisdoonvarna had signed a contract with the Irish Department of Justice to turn the hotel into a Direct Provision centre for asylum seekers arriving into Ireland.
>
> The reaction from the Lisdoonvarna community upon hearing this news was shock and deep suspicion of the secrecy involved especially when the town has previously been rejected as a suitable location to house a small number of Syrian refugees and their families.
>
> Lack of public services, minimal public transportation, over-crowding at the primary and secondary schools and crèche were noted, as just a few of the obvious drawbacks to the plan.

The community of Lisdoonvarna still have questions and would like an explanation as to why they were not consulted and able to make plans of their own to accommodate approx 30% increase in population to the locality of Lisdoonvarna.

The page has been created to provide information and assistance regarding the Direct Provision and to notify residents and visitors of Lisdoonvarna about any meetings and events that take place in regards to the new centre.

Lisdoonvarna is now the subject of an already controversial situation that has caused a lot of upset between different parties, please remember everyone has an opinion and we still need answers to our many questions, when commenting please be respectful to your current and new neighbours alike.

The following message was also posted:

This page has been created because many residents were unaware of last Friday's Public Meeting that was organised after the decision to incorporate a Direct Provision centre in Lisdoonvarna was leaked and became public knowledge.

Many residents did not attend because the meeting was not publicised effectively.

The meeting with the Owner of the Hotel and a Civil Servant from the RIA Reception and Integration Agency took place to address local residents and businesses about their intentions. Many people in the area have concerns regarding the effect that an immediate large increase of population will have on facilities and amenities in the area and also how the smaller businesses that rely on a tourist trade will be affected. But most of all, why there has not been a consultation process to prepare everyone, including local schools, medical services, An Garda Síochána and other public amenities in the area?

Many of the attendees were not aware of the term Direct Provision or the Asylum process before Friday and may still not have the information they might seek.

The meeting raised many points that had not been considered, even by the hotel owner who postponed the signing of his legal contract at the concerns of the community in attendance. Therefore another meeting was scheduled for Wednesday 28 February at 7 p.m. with representatives from the above-mentioned agencies. It is expected that the same questions will be raised again by residents that were unable to attend the first meeting due to work and personal commitments.

The meeting on Monday evening will be to plan and strategise an effective use of the limited time available on Wednesday evening to accommodate all of the questions raised.

Everyone is welcome to attend both meetings.

I was delighted to see leadership evolving. It was great to see all the necessary concerns being raised. Basic services, such as the doctor and schools, need to be able to support such a large population increase. I was intrigued by the statement about 'how the smaller businesses that rely on a tourist trade will be affected' and wondered why the Gardaí needed to be prepared.

I went along to the second community meeting on Monday 26 February with the intention of sitting quietly beside my friend to give her moral support. Over one hundred people attended to help prepare a list of questions for RIA, which was the advertised intention of the meeting notice. Soon after it started the meeting turned into a debate, bordering on an argument. There were concerns about our ability to cater for so many people, some blatantly racist comments, and some expressions of support for actions to help asylum seekers. After about fifteen minutes of agitated discussion and the airing of opposing views and raised voices I asked if anyone was writing up the questions. There was no reply. Given that nobody was taking questions and that I was there with a notebook and pen, I ended up taking the microphone and facilitating the rest of the meeting. I noticed my best friend and her daughter up near the front and smiled at them, assuming she had been silent all week because she had been busy.

People had a lot to say and a cocktail of emotions created strong tension in the hall. It took me a minute to adjust to the role, as I had to come up with a strategy that respected everyone's right to speak in the heated environment. I had qualified as a mediator the previous year, so that helped. I asked that people frame what they had to say as a question and everyone who wanted to speak was given the opportunity. It was a long meeting and went on until 11 p.m. but by the end of the evening the mood was determined and there was a shared sense of achievement. When I left, my best friend and her daughter were still in the car park. I went over to them but they turned away as I approached, glanced at me and started to laugh as they walked away.

My mind was racing and I was pretty hyper when I eventually got home, so I sat up for another few hours. I condensed everything I had written at the meeting into 36 questions. They ranged from concerns about the contract to infrastructure, facilities, the Direct Provision system itself and the asylum seekers.

I was getting a good sense of the community response and initial reactions to the proposal were very varied. Some people were totally opposed to the idea – they were horrified that a local hotel would be used to house asylum seekers and feared that it would wreck the town's reputation. Some people used examples of lawlessness in Germany to illustrate the potential trouble it could bring. Others were concerned that the population increase would result in services such as education and healthcare being stretched and that their own children would suffer. There was anger about how the people of Lisdoonvarna had found out about the plans and that the decision was out of their hands, as the community had no say.

Many people had sympathy for the asylum seekers, and some stated that they could imagine themselves in the same situation someday, or drew parallels with the Irish 'famine'. Most who attended acknowledged that those seeking asylum hadn't caused the situation. There was a lot of willingness to ensure they were warmly welcomed and well cared for.

On 27 February, the following message was posted by the administrator in the Direct Provision Lisdoonvarna Facebook group. While it contains the questions I had compiled following the town hall meeting, I did not write the accompanying dialogue. The answers are included in Appendix 1.

Meeting Minutes - Monday 26 February 2018

Approximately 100 members of the Lisdoonvarna community met for more than two hours in the Pavilion to discuss the proposed transformation of the historic hotel into a Direct Provision centre for asylum seekers arriving in Ireland. The Irish government put out a tender offer for suitable facilities in early January 2018, which the hotel owner applied for. He was informed earlier this month that he had won the contract and that 115 asylum seekers would begin moving into the hotel on Monday 5 March 2018.

The town learned of this very late last Tuesday, essentially through a news leak to the Lisdoonvarna Fáilte. At a hastily arranged town meeting on Friday morning with the hotel owner and an official from the Reception and Integration Agency, tempers ran high and many questions went unanswered.

As a result, the official promised to return to Lisdoonvarna in order to answer every question on Wednesday 28 February, along with representatives of An Garda Síochána, HSE, Department of Education and Department of Justice.

Monday's meeting was organised by the people of Lisdoonvarna to prepare for Wednesday's meeting.

At the Friday meeting the hotel owner also said that he would follow the wishes of the people of Lisdoonvarna if they disagreed with this change of use.

Monday's meeting reflected many points of view, but the basic emotion from every person there was sympathy for asylum seekers and a desire to take the best humanitarian action. However, there were differences among attendees, ranging from practical opinions about protecting Lisdoonvarna's reputation as an international tourist destination and maintaining property values, to passionate defence of the importance of international charitable support, regardless of the cost. There was also a lot in between, including reminders that Lisdoonvarna could benefit a good deal, as the government appears willing to invest large sums in asylum seekers who they settle here. A serious topic that arose several times is the relative failure of the Direct Provision system over the last twenty years. There is ample evidence that the system is disliked by clients and providers alike.

After an hour and a half of comments and observations, attendees formulated specific questions for Wednesday night, which are detailed below to provide time to research complete answers. Several questions emphasise the apparent lack of transparency (and honesty) in the government's statements so far about the situation

Another topic, probably the most important, is how Lisdoonvarna will answer the hotel owner's offer to abide by the town's wishes.

By having plainly stated on Clare FM radio and several times at the Friday morning meeting that he would act in accordance with the town regarding the future of establishing a Direct Provision centre in the hotel, the owner seemed to have pledged a willingness to back away from the contract with the Department of Justice.

Or did he? And how will he be informed if this project is supported by the town or not?

There were clear differences of opinion among those attending the meeting.

The need for a vote among the community to make this decision was reluctantly agreed to. It was decided that it would be a Yes or No vote or cap on numbers being accommodated and that it would take place on Wednesday night after the questions were answered.

A secret and secure ballot will be designed.

Everyone from the entire parish (Lisdoonvarna, Doolin, Kilshanny & Toomevara) is urged to attend. Bring a recent utility bill with your home address if there is a chance that you are not in the official voter registry.

This is an important step in the long history of Lisdoon-varna. The conflict of supporting the world's suffering souls while potentially losing our livelihood as a tourist centre is paramount. The fear of being criticised for being strong enough to stand up to a national government that has bullied and shamed many Irish towns into supporting their sometimes misguided and clearly mismanaged policies on refugees is daunting.

Please attend on Wednesday and let your voice be heard. Bring family and friends and neighbours. And let us all hope that this can be an opportunity for Lisdoonvarna to grow together, for the good.

Questions raised:
» Logistical questions about the contract.
» Is the contract signed?
» Who decided Lisdoonvarna would be a host village?

» Does the hotel owner still own the hotel or has it been sold recently?

» Who is expected to sign a contract to feed and care for the asylum seekers?

» Is there a per capita cut-off on numbers housed? We would have the highest ratio of locals to asylum seekers in the country.

» Why were we not consulted before last week? Why the secrecy?

» Can the implementation be put back a few months?

» Is the second group of 30 being deferred, as promised?

» Can the allocation be capped at 30?

» We require a review committee be put in place to include four members of the Lisdoonvarna community, four members of the Direct Provision centre, one HSE rep, one Department of Education rep, one Department of Justice rep ... who else?

» There was a lot of concern about the Direct Provision system itself.

» Will the asylum seekers be housed in Lisdoonvarna without support?

» Will they be provided healthy, balanced meals?

» Will their participation in community activities be funded – equipment, gear etc?

» Will they receive counselling for psychological issues arising from their experiences?

» Could there be opposing groups housed in the centre? Enemies?

» What provision is there for language to enable integration?

» Can the residents cook for themselves?

» Do the residents have basic family time, such as sitting down to a meal together?

» What will be done to stop them suffering from being stuck in a hotel?

» Can the residents work?

» How do residents integrate elsewhere?

» Questions about the people themselves.

» Are there any asylum seekers who have been refused admission elsewhere? In the UK?

» What nationality are they?

» Are they all families? How many are in family units?

» What is the age breakdown? Concerns about concentration of one age group, especially young males and orphans.

» Concern about facilities and infrastructure.

» Will our schools be supported and given the resources and facilities they need?

» Will we get another doctor? Most doctors in North Clare are at capacity.

» Will we have more Gardaí and the station open?

» What about the population increase and support for new parents amongst the asylum seekers?

» Will our health centre have additional support?

» Will our transport service be improved? There isn't much to do in Lisdoonvarna and they may wish to go further afield.

» Will they have help with language at school and other services?

» What religions will need to be accommodated? Are there facilities?

» These questions will be followed by a Yes or No vote by those who attend – all welcome from the Parish of Lisdoonvarna & Kilshanny (this area includes Lisdoonvarna, Doolin, Kilshanny & Toovahera).

» NB In order to vote you must be on the register of electors for the parish – Lisdoonvarna, Doolin, Kilshanny &

Toovahera. Or bring an official document, bill or bank statement with your address being within those areas. Arrive at 6.30 p.m. to register to vote.

This Facebook post raised many questions for me. While it had been mentioned the previous evening, I didn't know who had decided to hold a vote. Why would Lisdoonvarna's reputation as an 'international tourist destination' need protecting? What was going to damage it? Why would property values need maintaining? There were more questions about people's country of origin and religion and about increased Garda numbers for the village. Nationality and religion were clearly a focus of some of the community's concerns.

It was becoming obvious that a lot of propaganda was being shared and much of it was coming from sources outside of Lisdoonvarna. Social media was being used to spread hate messages with videos claiming to prove asylum seekers and certain religious groupings were lawless in other countries. There were stories circulating that property prices would plummet, business would dry up and no woman or child would be safe to walk the streets. Racist fears were being manufactured. We had the attention of the far right. The 'far right' get their name for pursuing a right-wing agenda to the extreme by being more conservative, nationalistic and authoritarian than the 'right' or 'centre right'.

Personally, I had broken my new year's resolution to avoid voluntary work for a while. Within a week of the news breaking I was standing in front of people I hardly knew. I was bringing some calm and structure to a chaotic situation where everyone was in uncharted waters. This was the night that I took on a role of facilitating the community response to the proposed Direct Provision centre in Lisdoonvarna. I had been living in Lisdoonvarna for less than three years and my community was obviously struggling with this news. As an experienced community development facilitator and mediator, I had the relevant skills and experience, so I stepped up. But I hadn't anticipated how emotionally difficult the whole experience would be.

14

Media Frenzy

The media attention was pretty intense. I had missed the first few days and initial bombardment but once I stepped up, I found myself in the spotlight. Others had played that role for the first while but they were now sending media enquiries in my direction. It wasn't a daunting task for me as I was happy to take it on to help out. I had completed many strands of media training, including television, radio and written.

Here is some of the media coverage. It comes from a variety of sources and interviews with numerous people:

Radio

The local radio station, Clare FM, was hopping with news and updates from the unfolding story in Lisdoonvarna. From what I can see they were first in for interviews with locals, the hotel owner, business owners and community representatives.

The first report from Clare FM came on Wednesday 21 February, the day after the news broke. Many people in Lisdoonvarna listened to the radio and this was some of the news they were hearing. The following was posted on their website on 21 February.

> Lisdoonvarna Hotel to Accommodate Asylum Seekers
>
> The Department of Justice has confirmed that a Lisdoonvarna hotel is to accommodate asylum seekers from next month.
>
> The Department has told Clare FM that the Hotel in Lisdoonvarna will house asylum seekers, or what it calls 'applicants for international protection' with effect from March 5th.
>
> Their statement to Clare FM does not say how many will be accommodated there, but the Hotel, which is located on the outskirts of Lisdoonvarna, has 65 en-suite bedrooms.

The Department recently sought expressions of interest for such accommodation, given what it calls 'significant pressure' on space in the system.

It also says that it is grateful for the support of local communities around the country where these centres are located.

Efforts to contact the owner of the Hotel have so far been unsuccessful.

On Thursday 22 February, the Clare FM Morning Focus radio show conducted interviews with various parties and seemed to aim to include all sides of the story. The issue was proving very divisive. Not all Lisdoonvarna residents were happy hearing others speaking on their behalf, especially when they weren't from the area themselves. It was very emotive and resulted in some listeners attending meetings and getting involved. While Clare FM took a balanced approach, that wasn't the case for other radio stations.

I was used to speaking about my areas of interest and expertise, including climate change, public participation and environmental matters. My focus at that time was the response of my community to the non-consultative process in which a contract was being imposed on our village.

One morning I participated in a radio interview with a presenter who pushed me quite aggressively on the Direct Provision system in Ireland. I had never claimed to be an expert on Direct Provision, as I was just facilitating the community response. However, that morning I found myself on air with a man who used the conversation to talk about asylum seekers working illegally and how everyone 'knew it'. He seemed to just want to channel negativity towards asylum seekers.

I remember it as a sunny day. I got off the phone feeling like I had just been interrogated and attacked. I replayed the interview in my head and the more I thought about it, the more attacked I felt. Eventually I just burst into tears as I sat alone in my kitchen, having just been used to spread negativity about people I hadn't even met. I was sure the radio presenter hadn't met them either, but I felt that he happily stoked the fires of racism.

I wanted to ring my best friend, but she had made it very obvious that we were no longer friends, so instead I rang the person who had sent the radio station my way and discussed the interview with them. I needed to talk to someone who was in touch with the situation just to share the experience. I doubt he realised how upset I was, but telling him what had happened helped me to deal with it. We also used the opportunity to discuss some parameters for future media interactions. We agreed we would not allow ourselves to be used to enable attacks on asylum seekers, or on anyone, for that matter.

The local paper

The following is one of numerous articles that appeared in one local newspaper, *The Clare Champion*. It provides good insight into the mood and what was being said at the time, and how it was heard by the media.

> Heated views at Lisdoonvarna Direct Provision public meeting
> 23 February 2018
>
> A public meeting, addressing the opening of a Direct Provision centre in Lisdoonvarna on March 5, was attended by approximately 100 people at the Pavilion in the town on Friday morning.
> The meeting heard stringent criticism from many speakers who questioned whether Lisdoonvarna was equipped to cater for up to 115 asylum seekers, approximately 30 of whom are due to start living there on the first Monday of next month. While some speakers said that they would like to help the asylum seekers, many maintained that the town, which has a population of 300 people, does not have sufficient health, educational or social services to cater for the prospective new arrivals.
> However, some doubt was cast on the future of the Direct Provision centre in the town when the Hotel proprietor said

that he had yet to formally sign the contract and that he would listen to the views of local people, before making a definite decision.

The Principal Officer with RIA, told The Clare Champion after the meeting, that he expects the Direction Provision centre to open.

'I wouldn't accept there is no final decision. From my perspective we have concluded our discussions with the contractor. We hope and expect that we will have people in the accommodation centre on March 5 but as I said at the meeting we will meet here again on Wednesday evening with all the service providers in the area to reassure the people that those who are coming into Ireland, seeking international protection, will be afforded a North Clare welcome. We want to assure that the services and supports already here won't be diminished but will be added to,' he said, noting that he expects the owner to sign the contract.

'I don't see the non-signing of it as being a major issue. If it happens for some reason, then we can't do it but I don't expect at all that to be the case. I hope I addressed as many of the questions as I possibly could today. This will be the 35th accommodation centre that we will have opened up across the country. The state agencies involved are well used to this business. The schools, educational and health services are able to step up to the mark and are able to deliver. I can absolutely understand the fears and apprehensions of the townspeople in relation to this but I can assure them all that we will deliver,' he stated.

He defended his department's communication of the news to the residents of Lisdoonvarna. Most local people heard the news on Wednesday of this week.

'You have to understand where we're coming from. On January 8 we published an advertisement in the papers seeking accommodation. We got upwards of twenty responses. We analysed them and we inspected the premises in question here. It's suitable and it meets our needs. As soon as we concluded our contractual discussions, which was at the end of last week, we finished off the paperwork at the beginning of this week. Then we contacted all the TDs, Senators and local councillors on Tuesday at lunch time. I don't think we could have done it any faster. The bottom line is that we have to provide for the people who are seeking international protection,' he asserted. ...

National media

The story was reported in most national newspapers, radio stations and on television. Before any asylum seekers arrived, the state news channel, RTÉ, met a group of local people at my home and conducted some interviews. We were under the spotlight as the latest community to reject Direct Provision. RTÉ wanted to meet people involved in welcoming the asylum seekers and I wondered if anyone would be confident enough to pledge support on camera. I was pleasantly surprised by the five enthusiastic volunteers who stepped up at short notice. A plan to make cards and put together welcome packs at the kitchen table proved a nice backdrop for the interviews. The volunteers were even happy enough to speak on camera. I didn't feel so alone this time.

By mid-March we were getting a lot of attention from the far right, so a team from the current affairs programme *Prime Time* came to Lisdoonvarna. They investigated the reaction of the local community and reported on the role the far right was playing in stoking racism and fear. Earlier in March a group of people had come to Lisdoonvarna and had distributed leaflets to warn locals about the threat that asylum seekers posed.

The 'Diversity Crimes in Ireland' leaflet read: 'This open borders experiment has consequences. We should have strict vetting and a fast-track deportation system for those who commit crimes in our country.'

It listed rapes and murders reportedly committed by foreign nationals in Ireland over the past number of years. The group handed the leaflets to people as they walked into the hall for bingo and went into pubs. One manager noticed the group talking to customers, who seemed very uncomfortable with the situation. When he saw the leaflet he was furious and sent them away.

Online opinion

There was a massive online conversation across Twitter and Facebook. Twitter was the platform most used by businesses and tourism networks in the Lisdoonvarna area at the time, while Facebook was popular with the wider community. YouTube also played a role in the online opposition campaigns, with dedicated videos produced over time, on top of the racist content that already existed and was being distributed widely.

Some locals used social media to express their views, mostly Facebook. Attitudes were mixed, but I was taken aback by some very racist comments that were posted. I surveyed people in Lisdoonvarna in 2019 to capture their impressions during various stages of the process and one person recalled 'what was said online, on Facebook especially, was disgusting and it was said by people that have immigrated themselves to Lisdoonvarna and the surrounding areas. They were no way welcoming or understanding or had any compassion for the immigrants coming to Lisdoonvarna.'

Some people shared horror stories, videos and reports of vandalism, rape and riots in other countries, which were allegedly caused by asylum seekers and non-nationals. As one person put it, 'I heard of "black gangs of men with big knives" – those sorts of stories that are peddled by the gutter media.' The usual 'coming in here, taking our jobs and our land' attitude blossomed. People posed questions and imagined scenarios that painted the introduction of asylum seekers and refugees as something negative. Someone recalled, 'I found it quite upsetting and could not believe the anger and total disregard for the people that have no choice but to go where they are not wanted or welcomed'. I've included feedback from the survey throughout the book.

Common prejudices included the idea that there would be a threat to children's safety; increases in crime; decreases in tourism income and a lowering of property prices. There was also the 'what about our own' argument. Ireland has thousands of homeless people, so why weren't we helping them first? Why were asylum seekers being accommodated when Irish people have been on housing lists for years? People who demonstrated any tendency to support helping asylum seekers were inundated with all of these explanations for why it was a bad idea.

It was apparent that there were some people in Lisdoonvarna who had very racist views. Within weeks I had to block people on Facebook because they viciously attacked my posts and comments. By allowing them to comment on my posts I was only giving them a further platform for their hate and racist opinions. They used online conversations to exploit people's fears and the lack of information. I also reported a lot of Twitter accounts and Facebook posts. Twitter seemed to be the most responsive in dealing with the racist content, but no sooner was an account closed down than another one was immediately set up to replace it.

It was strange to be in the middle of this online struggle when I was still relatively new to the community. It was bizarre to have to block people I'd never met, who lived relatively close to me. I could be walking past them every day without realising it. For all I know they still harbour resentment. I will never know why my best friend rejected me but I accept the fact that she did not deserve the title of best friend.

> Our ability to reach unity in diversity will be the beauty and the test of our civilisation.
>
> Mahatma Gandhi

2

The Village that Voted No

The Night of the Vote

On Wednesday 28 February, the weather turned and we braced for the Beast from the East and storm Emma. The officials cancelled. That proved pretty useful because it gave us an opportunity to meet again as a community to run through the replies from the department and create another, new list of questions based on their answers. The number of attendees at our meeting would probably have been higher had the weather been better, as many people thought it had been cancelled. We were told that the meeting with officials would be rescheduled for the coming week but the rescheduled meeting never happened.

We were pretty frustrated with the lack of reliable information and it had become evident that a lot of people weren't familiar with Direct Provision. It was also evident that there were a lot of people who wanted to help those seeking refuge, regardless of the system in place.

The evening started with an introduction to the Direct Provision system, which was provided by Clare Public Participation Network (Clare PPN). I was a member of the Clare PPN secretariat or management team, but I wasn't well informed on the asylum process. She began by outlining the position of Clare PPN:

> At Clare Public Participation Network's plenary meeting, which took place on 30 November, 2017, those attending from Clare PPN's Social Inclusion College identified ending the system of Direct Provision and working to support those currently living in Direct Provision in Clare as one of the priority areas for Clare PPN in 2018.

She then read out the Clare PPN press release about the situation in Lisdoonvarna:

> Clare PPN secretariat decided that chairing a meeting between the community and those who wish to open a Direct Provision centre would compromise the position taken by its social inclusion members which committed Clare PPN to lending its support to efforts to end the system of Direct Provision in Ireland.
>
> Clare PPN would further recommend that communities should be fully informed and consulted on all plans that affect them and notes that consultations with relevant stakeholders such as schools, doctors and other service providers do not appear to have taken place in Lisdoonvarna. Representatives from Clare PPN attended the meeting which took place last night in Lisdoonvarna and noted that many people attending raised concerns that could easily have been addressed through proper planning, information sharing and consultation. Clare PPN calls on RIA and the Department of Justice to act in the interests of both asylum seekers and host communities to

ensure that the necessary services, staff vetting and resource provision take place before any attempt to relocate people to any area.

Our guest answered a lot of questions about Direct Provision. Her insight also helped to highlight important issues that any community should ensure are addressed in order to not add to the misery of the residents of a centre. This new information helped shape questions for the officials. It also helped people realise that this was no holiday for asylum seekers.

I then read out the questions gathered on Monday 26 February with the answers received from the RIA on Wednesday 28th. These are all contained in Appendix 1. We then prepared a list of follow-up questions. This second list of questions and the corresponding answers can be found in Appendix 2. Then we voted.

For the previous two days the thought of facilitating a vote that could be deemed racist had played havoc with my mind. I was aware of a loud racist element but knew that there were many people quietly waiting in the background to welcome asylum seekers. I had considered how it might play out and what I needed to do to protect my community from the harsh judgement of the external attention that was focused on us. I knew the wording of the vote would be vital so I left the logistics of the vote to others but said I would look after the wording of the ballot question. Those organising the vote got copies of the register of electors, ballot papers and a box. They were all set for the voting process.

In order to be democratic I consulted everyone at the meeting on the wording of the vote. I asked if people were opposed to asylum seekers in Lisdoonvarna, to which I got a resounding 'no'. Some people suggested that they would be open to a centre with fewer people. Others wanted more time to be involved in planning how Lisdoonvarna might accommodate asylum seekers properly. It was obvious that the contract was the issue.

It took twenty minutes or so to word the question in the Yes or No voting format and in the end we went with 'Do you want the proposed

Direct Provision contract?' Nobody objected to that and everyone was eager to vote. 197 people voted No, while fifteen voted Yes. Therefore the people of Lisdoonvarna who attended the meeting voted against the proposed Direct Provision contract. There were almost 1,800 people on the register of electors in the wider parish area and just over 200 voted. It was far from a high turnout. However, it was representative of those who attended.

Most mainstream news sources reported that it was the Direct Provision contract that had been voted against. Others, however, were happy to distort the facts. The *Irish Examiner* newspaper reported: 'Lisdoonvarna votes 93% against asylum seekers' – an incorrect interpretation that was also used by those who were pursuing a racist agenda. The far right used the vote as a great opportunity to stoke racism and continue to use the *Irish Examiner* article to misrepresent the facts.

Unbeknownst to most people attending the meeting, the vote had been recorded. I am aware of two different recordings, one of which was made by someone who had travelled to film it. This person has since gone on to fuel anti-immigrant sentiments in other communities across Ireland, including Wicklow, Rooskey, Moville, Oughterard, Achill Island and Ballinamore. He has moved on to live-streaming the far-right-fuelled anti-immigration protests from communities, including East Wall and Ballymun in Dublin in 2023. The recording of the vote was used to misrepresent my role in the community and support a conspiracy theory put forward by the far right, which asserts that individuals – moles – are planted within communities to collude with the government. They used the recording to claim that there are non-governmental organisations (NGOs) in this sector that actually work for the government. These claims are lies. I was not planted, and was not working for anyone or acting as a government mole – yet the people of Oughterard, for example, and possibly others, were later led to believe that I was.

As a facilitator at both meetings, I noted that there was a lot of compassion for asylum seekers. There was a lot of frustration and disbelief at the fact that this contract had been negotiated without our community's input or knowledge. I also noted fear and concern about how the centre would impact the town, especially education and health care services. The lists of questions clearly reflected the sentiments of the community. There was a lot of concern about the conditions that asylum seekers are expected to live in, the lack of public transport, the impact of placing 115 more people in a small town with a little over 800 inhabitants, and the total disregard for public participation in the planning.

Some people were of the opinion that we should look after our own first, which is a common argument against the Direct Provision system. The questions about nationality and religion were strategically answered by RIA. The 2016 census recorded that 35.5% of people who were already in Lisdoonvarna were not Irish. Of the 821 people in Lisdoonvarna who responded to this census question in 2016, only 481 identified as Catholic. I don't know of anyone else being asked about their religion or nationality when they moved in. I certainly wasn't.

The big unanswered question throughout both meetings was whether the owner of the hotel had actually signed the contract. His evasiveness did not do him, the community, or the asylum seekers any favours.

Lisdoonvarna had now voted no to the proposed Direct Provision contract. However, we still didn't know if that would have any impact on the government's or the hotel owner's plans. It didn't.

News eventually broke that the contract had been signed and asylum seekers would move in on 5 March. This demonstrates how the government and accommodation providers operate. News of the Direct Provision centre broke on 20 February and the first residents were to move in on 5 March – thirteen days later. However, due to the severe snowstorm, the first residents arrived a week later than planned. So on 12 March the Direct Provision centre opened its doors to asylum seekers, exactly twenty days after the community had first heard of the plan.

A couple of elected councilors attended the two community meetings I was at. They were in the audience and as far as I could make out were just picking up on whatever the popular sentiment was. They provided no leadership or guidance. There have been other instances since then in other communities where a Direct Provision centre has been proposed, where elected representatives have been blatantly racist. That's just not good enough. Many politicians are not equipped, trained or mandated to handle these situations. It has become clear that there are some people with extremely racist views in decision-making roles within our government.

In the absence of dedicated facilitators and capable leaders, why does RIA do what they do, causing chaos in communities? Is this part of their strategy – to divide and conquer? A good few people thanked me for facilitating both meetings and keeping everything on track. While I didn't expect or need the thanks, I was reassured that I was filling a necessary role that the government had failed to fill. There are now plans to end Direct Provision, but whatever replaces it must not be as shrouded in secrecy as the current system.

During the meetings, I gave everyone who wanted to an opportunity to speak. People were mostly respectful of each other's opinions and everyone was listened to. I put some shape on people's questions and while the list was long, it was inclusive of everyone's input. Most people said that they were opposed to Direct Provision but had a lot of empathy for the people fleeing their own countries. I'm sure many people in Lisdoonvarna had shed a tear at the sight of the drowned Syrian toddler Aylan Kurdi, who washed up on a Turkish beach on 2 September, 2015. I found it heartening when I heard people say that it's not that long since many of our own ancestors died at sea trying to reach America, Canada or Australia – anywhere safe during the Great 'Famine'. This happened around a dozen times, with mostly older people saying it.

In an attempt to help channel people's eagerness to act, I created two new Facebook groups on 5 March. One group I called 'Caring for Asylum Seekers in Lisdoonvarna'. The other group I called 'Lisdoonvarna Against Direct Provision'.

Within days there were almost 100 people in the Caring group. That number soon doubled. The purpose of the group was to share news from the centre and seek supplies that people might be able to share, such as prams, toys, uniforms, clothes, etc.

The group against Direct Provision peaked at 26 members, with hardly any activity.

Having had the opportunity to explore what Direct Provision means for residents as well as the host community, people had expressed a wish to change the system. It just so happens that as a systems analyst and activist who has engaged with national and local policy, having previously worked as a civil servant, changing the system is one of my favourite activities. I was fully prepared to work with people on this cause. There was support from Clare PPN, as they had made a statement outlining their opposition to Direct Provision and there were other groups we could liaise and collaborate with on a campaign. However, a campaign against Direct Provision never materialised in Lisdoonvarna.

Save Lisdoonvarna

As well as some locals drumming up fear and racism, far-right agitators came to our town and put out an SOS to the international community to save Lisdoonvarna from the 'Great Replacement'. Replacement theory is a white nationalist, far-right conspiracy theory that the white European population at large is being progressively replaced with non-European people. It is another conspiracy theory that is shared by the far right in Ireland. It aligns with the conspiracy theory that there is a 'Great Reset' being orchestrated by the 'New World Order'. A lot of these ideas come from QAnon in America and fascist groups across Europe.

Believers in the Great Replacement theory, including some Irish political parties, were delighted that Lisdoonvarna had voted no. Some visited Lisdoonvarna to try to drum up support for their cause while generating fear within the community. As well as distributing racist leaflets at bingo and in the pubs, they taped a poster to the door of the proposed Direct Provision centre that stated: 'Objection to the Great Replacement of Europeans will not be tolerated – Thank you for your compliance.' A photo of this poster, kindly provided by Eamon Ward, can be seen on page 29. It had a golden harp and a blue EU flag at the bottom. Those who believe

in these conspiracies are generally opposed to Ireland's membership of the European Union and consider themselves true nationalists or patriots.

Almost overnight, #Lisdoonvarna went from being a Twitter tourist destination to the centre of a massive conspiracy theory where the population was supposedly being 'replaced'. Twitter was filled with tweets about Lisdoonvarna and many are still there. A pattern emerged as the same few accounts tweeted constantly, tagging or linking Lisdoonvarna to racially motivated material, such as violence and crimes that they attributed to asylum seekers and refugees. They put out a call for help to save the poor Irish town from the 'Great Replacement'. What they were doing posed a real threat to the local economy, as the tourism season was on the horizon. Holidaymakers would see the online racism, conspiracies and propaganda associated with Lisdoonvarna while they searched for places to visit or stay – it wasn't very enticing.

Videos were also created to tell the tale. The Irish National Party came to Lisdoonvarna. The far-right NP is against the EU, immigration and abortion; it is pro-aristocracy, corporal punishment and the death penalty; their slogan is, 'Ireland belongs to the Irish'. In a video about

Lisdoonvarna they claimed to portray the 'firsthand accounts by locals in the town' without actually quoting or interviewing any locals on camera. They filmed the vote and went on to create a one-sided documentary called 'When Lisdoonvarna Said No'. They never made clear what Lisdoonvarna said no to. They claimed that the asylum seekers coming to Lisdoonvarna would not have been accepted in urban areas.

It just so happens that a former *Breitbart* editor has renovated an old cottage in Lisdoonvarna. The American-based *Breitbart News* is considered an 'alt-right' media platform. We had a founding father of the far-right media in our midst. I spoke on the phone with Mr B on 6 March ahead of a radio interview he participated in. He rang me from America and spent the call telling me how detrimental a Direct Provision centre would be to Lisdoonvarna and how Europe was being destroyed by this influx of migrants. That's effectively what he said during the radio interview, which was described in a *Breitbart* article that is discussed below.

For my part, I used the opportunity to tell him that I had more people offering to help asylum seekers than objecting. I explained how more people would be seeking refuge as the climate breaks down further and resource wars escalate. He wouldn't hear any of it. If I had magic powers and had known what he was going to say on the radio before speaking with him I could have helped him fact-check some of his claims before he went on air. There was a lot of disinformation, from the very start.

The article referred to him as a resident of a tiny Irish town whose locals were helpless against European Union immigration policies as Ireland had become a slave state of the EU. He claimed that locals feared being accused of racism as he went on to question where the asylum seekers were coming from and their religion. He then stated that the residents of Lisdoonvarna had voted against turning the hotel into accommodation for asylum seekers. This was another misrepresentation of the fact that people had voted against the *contract*, which had been agreed without their knowledge or participation.

The article went on to share how Mr B, a US citizen, had roots in Lisdoonvarna, which was described as isolated and traditional, while attracting many tourists to its matchmaking festival every year. He feared the village would dramatically change. Despite his concerns about being misrepresented as racist, he went on to generalise about asylum seekers. He argued that Ireland had become a slave state of Brussels and there were plans for mass migration to increase the population in the national development plan, *Ireland 2040*. His opinions align well with the Great Replacement theory.

The American link caused me some concern. Over 30 million people in America claim Irish ancestry and many have set ideas about our culture and lives. It is no secret that many Americans have supported and funded the Republican struggles in Northern Ireland. Being told that Ireland is once more under threat may awaken the Irish American sense of patriotism and encourage them to support his call. All well and good if they are supporting the community, but this was not a call from the majority. This was not the full version of events or full disclosure of facts. I don't know who heeded this call but I do know the far right has been more vocal since. I hope that Irish-American money is not going into supporting the far right and racism in Ireland.

On 8 March one of the two people who had recorded the vote visited the Clare PPN office. He recorded himself beforehand, while he was sitting in his car, and mentioned *Breitbart News*. He proposed a lot of theories and implied that I and others were somehow orchestrators who were being paid by the government to support the Direct Provision centre in Lisdoonvarna. He didn't record how his intrusion into the PPN office went because there was nothing to report. He was treated courteously and found nothing to support his accusations because they were fictitious.

His two-hour YouTube video about the 'asylum industry' insinuated that I and others had collaborated with the government in the 'Great Replacement' of Lisdoonvarna natives, and that I had been paid to do so. He focused on my role and made statements and suggestions about the funding of NGOs in an attempt to imply I was paid to assist the government in establishing Direct Provision centres. The fact is that I helped my community in a voluntary capacity. That didn't fit his narrative so he

31

created his own. He couldn't find any supporting evidence, so he had to insinuate that I had been paid.

This same individual then used the asylum industry video to fuel opposition to Direct Provision in Oughterard in County Galway in 2019. In his own words, Lisdoonvarna was where he 'first got familiar with this topic'. He also used stories and footage from Moville and Rooskey. I wonder why he was interfering. I wonder if he was paid to interfere. I wonder if he is still being paid to interfere and lie, considering he has shown up in communities at numerous proposed Direct Provision sites since. Who is funding his 'work'? Given the international call for support that *Breitbart* put out, is it coincidental that Lisdoonvarna was his first port of call? Was he invited to interfere?

He has gathered almost 9,000 subscribers on YouTube over the past three years by focusing on the Great Replacement; on HIV and Covid-19 being fake news; attacking Black Lives Matter, and trying to discredit anti-racist and anti-fascist efforts; conducting interviews with the National Party, the Irish Freedom Party and Irish far-right extremists; spreading baseless accusations of paedophilia about several individuals; and filming live from East Wall and and what he called the 'anti-plantation' protest in Ballymun. That means almost 9,000 people are listening to his propaganda.

The Inner Circle

On or around 6 March I was sent an email thread from a member of a group consisting of ten people who were busy behind the scenes. Most were involved with the community in a business or voluntary capacity and the former *Breitbart* editor was one of them. They had sought legal advice and were considering an injunction to block the Direct Provision plans. Amongst this group were some of the people who had expressed strong racist views online and at the meetings. I expect some people in the group might have become involved because they were concerned about how the addition of 115 people to the village would affect facilities and resources for the community.

In hindsight I realise how not being around for the first few days helped me with my facilitating role later. I was oblivious to what was going on behind the scenes with this group. They did not communicate publicly as a group, as far as I was aware. There was definitely nothing publicly available that detailed who they were or what they were discussing. They may have been behind the original Facebook information page called 'Direct Provision Lisdoonvarna Group'.

Had I known about them, I might never have gotten involved. I had naively facilitated the community response as I witnessed it and laid out two immediate paths that people seemed to be seeking. Despite the role I was playing I had not been invited to join this group, nor was I told of its existence until this late stage.

One message from the community at the time, which was reflected in the *Breitbart* article, was that the people of Lisdoonvarna did not want to object to the Direct Provision centre for fear of being called racist. This was stated in a way that framed the people of Lisdoonvarna as victims of a campaign to demonise them – that their valid objections were being labelled racist. Some people in this circle were the most vocal about objecting to being called racist yet they said things that were most definitely racist. Publicly, the message from some people was that they were opposed to Direct Provision; in reality, they were anti-asylum seekers.

The far right uses this as a manipulation tactic. They empathise with the people in a community who oppose Direct Provision. They create a common cause – in this case the fight against being labelled racist. The trouble with that is, they don't stop being racist.

By the time I understood the dynamics of this group I was aware of a campaign by the far right to fuel opposition to the Direct Provision centre and attack the people of Lisdoonvarna who had come forward to help welcome the asylum seekers into their community. I was aware of the Twitter onslaught and of the far right manipulating the facts. I was aware of their pleas to save Lisdoonvarna from the 'Great Replacement'. People had come into our village and distributed leaflets with racist stories of rape and murder. Videos were being made to undermine our community. I knew that there was a racist element in Lisdoonvarna and suspected that they had summoned reinforcements.

A large group of people in Lisdoonvarna were being silenced. From what I observed at the meetings and my conversations with locals I realised that it was actually the people of Lisdoonvarna sympathetic to asylum seekers who were being silenced, who were afraid to speak. The very reason I went to the second meeting was because a friend had asked me to join her. She had attended the fiery first meeting and had wanted to speak but hadn't. I joined her for the second meeting so she could speak in support of the plan. She didn't want to go alone. She wanted to help asylum seekers but was afraid to be on her own saying it. As time went on more and more people were quietly volunteering to help. These people were not on the email list of the inner circle.

It was looking more and more likely that this concern about being called racist, the 'victimisation of the community' only really bothered a handful of people. It was seeming ever more like a strategy to generate an 'us against them' campaign to bring people together to fight against being called racist. That is a message I have heard repeated at other Direct Provision sites since.

Having seen some of the inner circle's communications, concerned by the *Breitbart* presence, I decided to email them. I realise now that I may have unwittingly stopped them in their tracks. I received no replies. They didn't make themselves or their ideas known publicly and they may well harbour resentment about me interrupting their plans to seek an injunction. I seriously question what mandate they had to do so.

On 10 March, 2018 at 17:21 I sent the following response to an email thread in which they were discussing the injunction:

Hi folks

I just finished my blog. I'd guess that racism is something you may feel strongly about so I am sharing it with you in the hope that you will use all the resources you have available to you to help stamp out the racist element within our community. Besides what I have witnessed there have been some shocking stories coming from the schools, where children must have overheard conversations at home.

I was away for the first five days of the Direct Provision saga when the racism message went out. I accompanied a friend to the second meeting with the intention of observing and not getting involved. However, it was impossible to do nothing given what was happening. I had media training when I was a national spokesperson for the environment so I pulled together the position against Direct Provision, knowing that was the better message, including ensuring the vote reflected that message. I have been and remain happy to help with press releases and media. I considered pulling out of helping because some people deserve to suffer the consequences of their racism. That said, the rest of the population do not and that's the only reason I'm still involved.

Here is a quote from my blog:

This must stop here. By sending out this message, extreme right-wing, potentially dangerous people and groups have come to our community in person and online. People are more afraid of these individuals than they are of asylum seekers. I know that I am not the only one who feels more unsafe now than I have ever done in Lisdoonvarna. People are afraid to express their compassion and consideration for the people coming

35

next week. So this racist campaign is actually bullying our community.

I almost cancelled the photo shoot yesterday morning (*Irish Times* article) out of fear but what would that have achieved? It would have left little or no positive news for the article. Eventually I decided if these fascists threaten or harm me or my family it only proves that they are the actual enemy. I'm going to condense that – I was afraid of the people who have been invited into our community by the racist element who have summoned support.

You may also be interested in articles in the *Irish Times* and *Irish Mail* today. Some may even be proud.

I look forward to working with you all as we strive to make Lisdoonvarna an inclusive community.

Kind regards

Theresa

I heard nothing back nor any whisper of an injunction after that. It was not my intention to silence them because that doesn't really resolve anything. Participation is paramount and communication is key. I did want them to realise that the fear that was being generated within our community was real and it wasn't a fear of asylum seekers.

This is most of the article that was published in the *Irish Times* on 10 March, 2018 that I referred to in the above email:

We are against Direct Provision and how it was forced on us

Lisdoonvarna locals oppose centre amid concerns over far-right activity

Saturday 10 March, 2018, 01:45 Gordon Deegan

A sense of unease could be detected among locals in Lisdoonvarna this week ahead of the arrival on Monday of the first group of asylum seekers to be accommodated at a new Direct Provision centre in the north Co. Clare town.

Many people were reluctant to comment amid acrimony over how local opposition to the scale of the plan is being reported. There are also concerns over the arrival of members of a Dublin-based far-right group in the town in recent days with the aim of fomenting anti-immigrant sentiment.

'Three weeks ago if a tourist googled Lisdoonvarna, it was a wonderful place to go,' a local businessman said. 'Google it now and it is not positive because it is all bad stories about the Direct Provision centre that is being forced on us. We have had a bad run in the media.'

As preparations by a number of locals to welcome the first group of families continued on Friday, a leaflet was found taped to the red door of [the hotel] where the asylum seekers will be accommodated.

Complete with a Government of Ireland gold harp and a blue EU flag at the bottom, the leaflet stated: 'Objection to the Great Replacement of Europeans will not be tolerated – Thank you for your compliance.'

He described the placing of the sign on the door under the cover of darkness as 'sinister'.

Another anonymous leaflet distributed in the town documented various rapes and murders committed by foreign nationals in Ireland over the past number of years.

The 'Diversity Crimes in Ireland' pamphlet read: 'This open borders experiment has consequences. We should have strict vetting and a fast-track deportation system for those who commit crimes in our country... This list represents a small sample of a much larger problem.'

Looking at the leaflet, he said: 'That is not us in Lisdoonvarna. It is disgusting. We don't want that, but we seem to be getting it whether we like it or not.'

He added: 'The people in Lisdoonvarna are against Direct Provision and how it was forced on us; it has nothing to do with the people in Direct Provision. What these people [anti-immigration campaigners] have done is racist.'

The Dublin-based agitators were trying to 'hijack' local opposition to the new Direct Provision centre, which will have the capacity to accommodate 115 people.

'They [the campaigners] were telling me that they can help us out and do this and do that; their agenda is completely different,' he continued.

He said he came across members of the far-right group on Thursday night and asked them to stop asking customers in a Lisdoonvarna pub: 'Are you local? Are you local?'

Breitbart intervention

The arrival of the Dublin-based group coincided with the publication this week of a story on *Breitbart*, the US alt-right news platform, about a secret ballot vote in Lisdoonvarna in which 93 per cent of respondents said 'no' to the Direct Provision centre.

The *Breitbart* story was based on an interview with a Lisdoonvarna local, who was one of the founding editors of the alt-right platform. The author and screenwriter moved from the US to the Co Clare town a number of years ago and today lives in a renovated ancestral home there.

In the interview, he lamented Ireland being 'a slave state' of Brussels.

On the imminent arrival of the asylum seekers, he said: 'They won't tell us what country they're coming from. What religion they're from.'

In 2019 I asked people in Lisdoonvarna if they had experienced any racist sentiment from outside the community of Lisdoonvarna. In addition to responses I've already mentioned, this is what they said:

» Online, after the far right tried to get (incorrect) information about some of those who set up a team to help the asylum seekers. The amount of racist talk was some of the worst I'd ever witnessed.
» Yes. Lots. Especially on Facebook. It worries me how close they came to us.
» Yes, again a lot of discussion on Facebook and horrible comments about the people that were being put into the centre.
» Yes, the far right invaded the village for a few weeks.
» I am aware of certain outsiders distributing propaganda in the village. Didn't meet anyone directly.
» Yes. It wasn't very nice, either.

While we were struggling with the situation as a community, the far right were invading our village, physically and virtually, worrying people and distributing propaganda. They were filming us, distorting the facts, misrepresenting the community and making videos to suit their own racist agenda. This included official political parties established within the Republic of Ireland. We were afraid because we did not know who would be influenced by their propaganda or what they might do. A lot of this material is still available online, misinforming people.

> Pit race against race, religion against religion, prejudice against prejudice. Divide and conquer! We must not let that happen here.
>
> Eleanor Roosevelt

3

Caring for Asylum Seekers

The Facebook group 'Caring for Asylum Seekers in Lisdoonvarna' had over 50 members within a couple of days and doubled within a week or so. Some people were very committed to preparing a welcome of some sort. Others were very clear about wanting to be involved with whatever welcome was organised. We used Facebook, printed posters, the local radio, local papers, parish newsletters and word of mouth to let people know what was happening. Lots of people in the area got in touch with offers of toys, clothes and whatever else they thought might be useful. A local business offered their premises to store and sort donations.

We sought advice from the Clare Immigration Support Centre as to what would be best and they suggested we let people settle in for a few days before organising a welcome event. Aware that potential residents might have seen the media reports about a hostile community in Lisdoonvarna, we decided to leave little welcome packs in the centre to demonstrate that the community of Lisdoonvarna was open and welcoming. A group came together, made beautiful cards and created welcome packs including information booklets, some history books and a map of Lisdoonvarna.

Online Targets

We soon became aware of a targeted campaign opposing Lisdoonvarna welcoming the asylum seekers. A screenshot of the administrators page for the 'Caring for Asylum Seekers' Facebook group was posted to a far-right page and shared online. Readers of the far-right page were very nasty and speculated about the volunteers who were coordinating the welcome. In one very disturbing comment, the list of names in the screen-shot was likened to a hit list. Some volunteers were so frightened that they left the welcoming group and hid their Facebook profiles.

Screenshots of my Facebook page, as well as screenshots and posts from my blog, also circulated within far-right circles. Various people who were out to warn everyone about the 'Great Replacement' were not happy with our caring position. This was another time when I felt afraid. When you are living in rural Ireland, growing aware that the far right is drawing attention to you is concerning. Why would they want to harm me? I was just facilitating my community through tumultuous times caused by national policy that was unfit for purpose.

On 11 March, 2018, one of our group took screenshots of the far-right discussion about us. In order to alert others to what was going on we posted the screenshots into the Caring for Asylum Seekers group. We also posted a message asking that people be vigilant and not to give anyone directions to our homes.

We were obviously concerned for our safety and that someone could come looking for us at our homes. The screenshot images are shared in the coming pages.

We were being discussed on the Altview.ie Facebook page under a screenshot photo of the Caring for Asylum Seekers group admins.

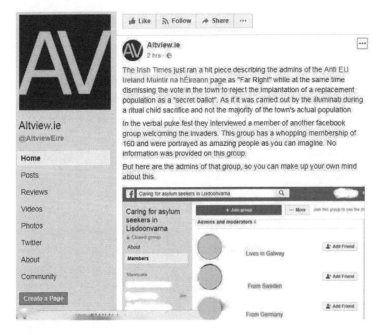

The post states:

> The *Irish Times* ran a hit piece describing the admins of the Anti-EU Ireland Muintir na hÉireann page as "Far Right" while at the same time dismissing the vote in the town to reject the implantation of replacement population as a 'secret ballot'. As if it was called out by the illuminati [sic] during a ritual child sacrifice and not the majority of the town's actual population.
>
> In the verbal puke fest [sic] they interviewed a member of another facebook [sic] group welcoming the invaders. This group has a whopping membership of 160 and were portrayed as amazing people as you can imagine. No information was provided on the group.

But here are the admins of this group so you can make up your own mind about this.

Someone had taken the picture, cross-referenced our Facebook profiles and gone on to write in our hometowns under our names in the screenshot.

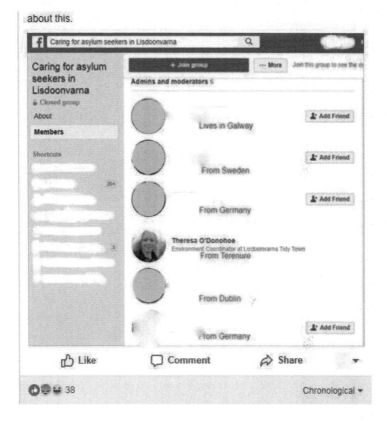

People were looking at who was in the group and commented that it was 'All local people then the admin'. There was a nice racist response to the fact that most of the admins were not Irish. 'The f*cking Germans... no surprises there... running their replacement population into Ireland', 'And Swedes...'.

They speculated that I have a holiday home in Lisdoonvarna as I am from Dublin and discussed how people move into a community and act like they own it.

They had a good look at my blog, where I report on my voluntary work regarding environmental policy in Ireland. I generally whistle blow on the lack of participation in policy- and decision-making in Ireland and advocate for changes to the current unbalanced, disjointed systems that are not fit for participation purposes.

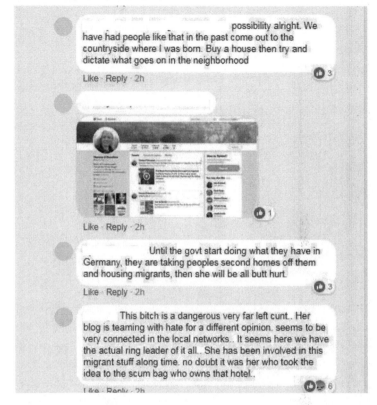

Then the venom really came out.

'This b*tch is a dangerous very far left c*nt. Her blog is teaming with hate for a different opinion. seems to be very connected in the local networks.. It seems here we have the actual ringleader of it all.. She has been involved with this migrant stuff along time. no doubt it was her who took the idea to the scum bag who owns that hotel..'

One person, sharing my blog post about the vote, then went on to say that I seemed to be the ringleader.

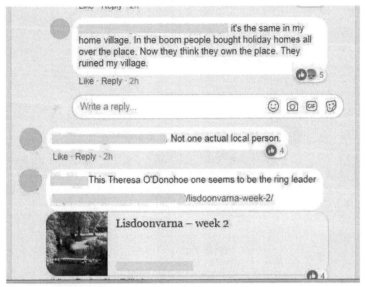

I write a blog called 'Building Bridges Between Policy and People'. I've been reporting for years on meetings I attend nationally and within Clare County Council, where I represent the environment and social justice in a voluntary capacity. I also write about public participation, climate and energy policy. I usually critique the system and highlight the lack of transparency, accountability and democracy. I report upon the deficit of consideration for collaboration or public participation in the civil service. I had written a blog post to report the systemic failure of these Direct Provision plans for Lisdoonvarna and what was happening. I shared the questions people had asked and the answers we received. My second blog on Lisdoonvarna exposed the antics of the far right.

The far right were interested in the Clare PPN position on Direct Provision. They copied the statement and link into a comment.

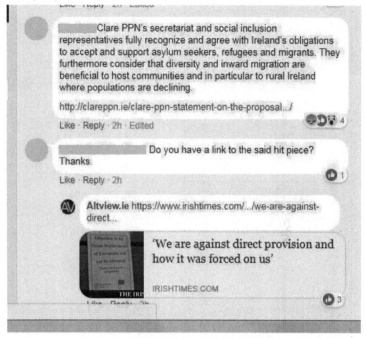

They also shared the *Irish Times* article about the interference of the far right, which included the piece about the welcome and a photo of those organising it.

They were really interested in me. Someone had seen elsewhere that they were puzzled by my blog because I recommended we infiltrate the system. It was ironic that they seemed to consider me an extremist.

Then one guy said it looked like a hit list. We feared that this could be embraced and acted upon by any one of them or someone else with extreme views. This was now a very scary situation for us.

They continued to speculate about the volunteers who had come forward to lead a welcome:

'Swedes and Germans who aren't content destroying their own countries doing the same to ours.'

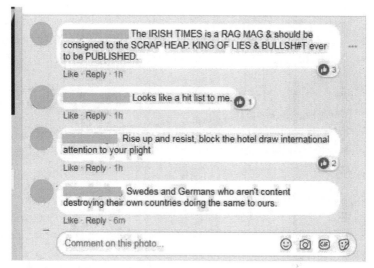

The IRISH TIMES is a RAG MAG & should be consigned to the SCRAP HEAP. KING OF LIES & BULLSH#T ever to be PUBLISHED.

Like · Reply · 1h   3

Looks like a hit list to me. 1

Like · Reply · 1h

Rise up and resist, block the hotel draw international attention to your plight

Like · Reply · 1h   2

, Swedes and Germans who aren't content destroying their own countries doing the same to ours.

Like · Reply · 6m

Comment on this photo...

All of a sudden, we found ourselves under personal attack from the far right. A racial attack at that, given their attitude towards the volunteers, who were mostly not Irish. Thirty-five per cent of Lisdoonvarna's population were not Irish.

There was a massive far-right conversation being had online about the situation in Lisdoonvarna. Sympathy and support were being sought for the little Irish community that was being left to its own devices to fight off this invasion. All sorts of scaremongering was going on, adding to the theory that there was a Great Replacement being orchestrated by the 'powers that be'.

It all made for pretty serious intrusions and a strong focus on us. Some of the organisers and members of the Caring for Asylum Seekers group left. People who had been very supportive but were vulnerable in rural Ireland decided to step away from helping. We told people not to give anyone directions to our homes or other admins' homes and to let us know if anyone was asking about us in the village. We changed the Facebook group settings from open to secret. We continued to prepare a welcome.

It was reported to the Gardaí, who could do nothing. The European Commission against Racism and Intolerance (ECRI) reports concerns about a lack of legislation to deal with hate speech in Ireland:

> The Prohibition of Incitement to Hatred Act 1989 is seldom used and is particularly ineffectual in combating online hate speech. Hate speech involving verbal abuse in public places is quite common. There is an undercurrent of low-level racist violence which is not adequately recorded or addressed.

The Irish current affairs programme *Prime Time* came down to investigate. Their show on 27 March, 2018 was very informative, highlighting the former *Breitbart* editor with a holiday home in the area who was calling for international opposition and seeking support to block the plans. The *Irish Times* reported that he was local. However, at the time he was living in America and visited Lisdoonvarna only occasionally.

This whole situation left me feeling very exposed, isolated and vulnerable. I was a single parent, relatively new to the area and my closest friend had dropped me. However, I met supportive people over the course of the following weeks and that network proved very important. We were all busy dealing with the attack on our efforts and digesting our own experiences. Thankfully, we had each other.

> First they came for the socialists, and I did not speak out because I was not a socialist.
> Then they came for the trade unionists, and I did not speak out because I was not a trade unionist.
> Then they came for the Jews, and I did not speak out because I was not a Jew.
> Then they came for me and there was no one left to speak for me.
>
> Martin Niemöller

4

Inside the Far Right

The far right in Ireland is being built on disinformation, deception and regression, while increasingly using online platforms to recruit supporters. Knowing who they are, or at least what to look out for, is half the battle in protecting our democracy. State intervention is vital.

I never understood the 'left' and 'right' labels in politics. Having become the focus of far-right attention I had to find out about these basics – the 'far right' and fascism. The political terminology of 'right' and 'left' was first used during the French Revolution in the eighteenth century, as politicians sat in parliament. Those to the right were supportive of the institutions of the monarchist regime and those to the left wanted the institutions changed.

Right-wing politics tend to be described as being conservative; seeking to preserve existing conditions, institutions and systems as much as possible. Someone with right-wing political views would generally view social inequality as normal, inevitable or possibly desirable. Much like the thinking of the French monarchy.

The further right you go, the stronger the emphasis on private ownership, personal wealth and individualism. People with right-wing political views believe that the resulting inequalities are the natural outcome of traditional social differences or competition in market economies. Fascism is a particularly aggressive, authoritarian and ultranationalist far-right political stance that involves racism and the oppression of others.

The right wing today advocates for the capitalist economy where the industry, business and services of a society are run by private individuals or for-profit companies. This chapter touches on the intersectionality, or cross-over, between right-wing politics, capitalism, racism, homophobia, fascism and extreme right-wing views. We also take a peek inside some of the conversations of the right.

Competitive economies have definitely created a lot of inequalities. Colonisation has shaped the world as countries have, throughout history, been invaded for their resources. The principle of 'every man for himself' is what led to Indigenous American people being moved off their land so that others could move in and use their resources. In 1884 the continent of Africa was carved up in the so-called Scramble for Africa and divided up by thirteen European countries. People across the globe continue to try to fight off those seeking to capitalise upon their resources. The profit does not go to those who were slaughtered, thrown out or bought out for pittance. The underlying assumption is that some lives matter less than others.

These right-wing ideologies are connected to each other and are connected to global migration patterns throughout history. That includes Ireland's mass migration, when the healthy crops grown here were exported to feed others, while indigenous people fled or died of starvation. This genocide is often incorrectly referred to as the Irish or Great 'Famine'. The belief that some people are more valuable than others is a foundation for injustice and a right-wing position.

Nationalism is a right-wing ideology that basically involves believing that one's country and people are superior to others. This is not the same as a love for one's country. Nationalists have rules about who can call their country home in the first place. The far right see integration with other cultures as a threat to their sense of identity. They reject the concept of diversity and see those of different races or cultures as a threat to their country and cultural values. This can lead to unrest within communities and prejudice toward those not deemed to share the same racial or cultural background. This prejudice often extends to sex, religion and other differences.

The far right came to Lisdoonvarna on the attack. We were targeted, trialled by Facebook and deemed the enemy because we cared about asylum seekers, fellow human beings who were in need. They detest difference and are fuelled by intolerance and hostility towards others they judge as being outside of their shared identity. They are building fear and division throughout Ireland by encouraging people to oppose asylum seekers.

Many of the far-right agitators who hounded us about Direct Provision in Lisdoonvarna appeared across Ireland as new sites were proposed. They turned up in Moville, County Donegal, in Roosky, Roscommon, in Lismore, Waterford and also in Wicklow. Two of those sites were subjected to arson attacks. Someone decided that burning the premises was better than housing people in need.

Nineteen months after Lisdoonvarna, the town of Oughterard in Galway was considered for a Direct Provision centre. The following excerpt is taken from an *Irish Times* article posted on Monday 23 September 2019:

> How the far right is exploiting immigration concerns in Oughterard.
>   Anti-immigrant activists trying to dominate and exploit local debates on Direct Provision
>   by Conor Gallagher and Sorcha Pollak
>   ...
>   'Asylum industry'
>   Initially, some people in Oughterard, including one of the main organisers, appeared to welcome outside

anti-immigration voices. Now they want to exclude them, fearing that they will be tarred by association.

One of the main agitators travelling to towns earmarked for Direct Provision or asylum housing is *M, a Cork man, who has visited Oughterard, Lismore, Lisdoonvarna and Roosky.

M frequently promotes far-right talking points on social media, particularly a conspiracy theory claiming the aim of western governments is to replace native populations with immigrants for economic reasons.

In a now-deleted tweet, M describes his political views as 'probably somewhere between libertarianism and national socialism with a touch of Christian ethos'.

In 2017 he posted a series of tweets expressing sympathy for white nationalists marching in Charlottesville in the US. Following the march, during which an anti-racism protester was murdered by a neo-Nazi, M posted: 'I can't imagine how surreal and frankly terrifying it felt for WNs in Charlottesville. And while I obviously don't condone the car attack...'

A two-hour YouTube video from M criticising the Government and the 'asylum industry' was widely shared in Oughterard and praised by some as 'a one-stop shop' for information about Direct Provision.

Such towns, he says, should 'identify and marginalise' Government-connected moles, subverters and intimidators within their ranks 'who are lurking among you.'

Advising locals to engage in Machiavellian thinking, he states: 'They can have no part in this discussion about your community. And they certainly should not be representing you and speaking for you.'

Public meetings are useful, too, to drum up support, especially if they are video-taped, and shared online. His advice, he says, was given in Rooskey, and it worked.

A local businessman who helps lead the 'Oughterard says No to inhumane Direct Provision centres' campaign initially praised the video which he called, in a Facebook post, 'extremely factual and well put together'.

M filmed the Oughterard meeting, capturing an Independent TD's declaration that African asylum seekers are sponging 'off the system here'.

...

Meanwhile, in Oughterard campaign leaders say the vigil outside the Connemara Gateway Hotel will continue and insist the help of the far right is not welcome.

'We have always welcomed people of all races and creeds,' the businessman said in a WhatsApp message last week accompanying a photo of a local restaurateur who is from Morocco, bringing food to the protesters.

'We are making a stand for something that is right and we have the people behind us.'

*M filmed the vote in Lisdoonvarna and created the two-hour video, which was deemed 'extremely factual and well put together' by a protester in Oughterard. This is the 'documentary' insinuating that I am a paid mole, working for the government. That lie is the reason I decided to write this book.

The internet was integral to communications around the community response in Lisdoonvarna. While it was a useful tool for those sharing vital information, organising meetings and welcomes, it was also used by the far right to pick and choose who to contact, find out where meetings were being hosted, decide who to target and generally find out what was going on in our community.

Social media offers a platform where information goes viral. Videos claiming to be footage of lawless asylum seekers robbing and rioting spread far and wide. The world wide web does not have an inherent, all-knowing, built-in fact checker. Nor does it have a conscience. Social media will show us anything it thinks we will look at or listen to. There are regulations and some protections to eliminate pornography or graphic images, certain words or phrases and whatever programming a platform mandates.

But ultimately the software is designed to give the consumer what they want and position relevant advertising in their space. If we read a certain opinion or 'fact' the software will automatically send us similar opinions, information and sources in the future to keep us engaged. It will also send us information based on our conversations, texts and emails. In theory it all seems pretty harmless. Until it is used to spread misinformation and lies.

The internet is a universe of information, celebrated for broadening the mind. Social media, however, has become a tool that can do the opposite. As social media platforms assess our needs, likes, beliefs, tastes, desires and so on, they flood our devices with them. They suggest friends, videos, groups and forums of like-minded people.

Pretty soon, we are immersed in a one-sided conversation where our friends say all the same things as us. We are fed the same information they are. Memes, videos, cartoons and articles reinforce our beliefs and others tell us that alternative stories are false. We become convinced that we are seeing the truth – there is no believable alternative!

The coming pages contain screenshots of some conversations conducted online in the spring of 2018. Conversations and forums like these helped shape some opinions at the time. I took the screenshots from an online, far-right forum where Lisdoonvarna was discussed in depth. Other topics included in the conversation are same-sex couples and abortion. The people of Ireland voted on both of these issues and it's quite clear from this forum that the people contributing here are out of touch with the population of Ireland and do not respect the democratic decisions we made.

Before news broke about Direct Provision in Lisdoonvarna, the National Planning Framework was being discussed on this far-right website. They felt that 'Ireland 2040' supports their belief that a Great Replacement is being orchestrated by the 'powers that be'. Many of their conversations seem to be framed around an underlying message that Ireland's cultural heritage is threatened.

The rest of the posts are from a long discussion thread about Lisdoon-varna. I have chosen some relevant posts. To start, someone set out the news about what was happening.

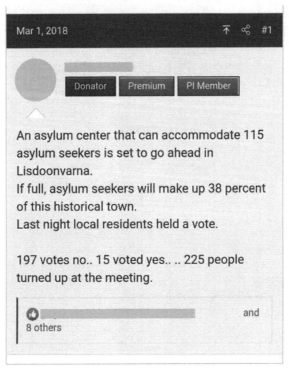

Mar 1, 2018   #1

Donator   Premium   PI Member

An asylum center that can accommodate 115 asylum seekers is set to go ahead in Lisdoonvarna.
If full, asylum seekers will make up 38 percent of this historical town.
Last night local residents held a vote.

197 votes no.. 15 voted yes.. .. 225 people turned up at the meeting.

and
8 others

This post reports the vote but fails to mention that people voted against the Direct Provision contract. It also mentions 'this historical town'. What does that actually mean? Is it some romantic reference to Ireland's cultural heritage? Ironically, Lisdoonvarna is a pretty new settlement, only established in the early nineteenth century.

Someone shared a well-worded tweet with a video of the vote. Using words like 'rejection', 'unanimous', 'sane', 'small town' and the #SaveLisdoonvarna hashtag. We came across the same tactic over and over, the consistent omission of what the vote was for. The far right would not clarify that the vote was against the Direct Provision contract. It is all done to mislead the reader into believing that the people of Lisdoonvarna rejected asylum seekers, which is a lie.

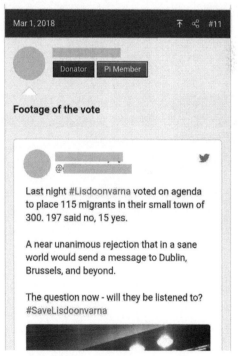

Mar 1, 2018   #11

Donator   Pi Member

Footage of the vote

Last night #Lisdoonvarna voted on agenda to place 115 migrants in their small town of 300. 197 said no, 15 yes.

A near unanimous rejection that in a sane world would send a message to Dublin, Brussels, and beyond.

The question now - will they be listened to? #SaveLisdoonvarna

Plenty of opinions were aired. Myths that opening a Direct Provision centre would destroy our village; house prices and tourism were repeated to create fear in local businesses and homeowners. Yet these fearmongers also imply that Lisdoonvarna is a venue for 'randy old farmers'. That's hardly a solid tourism strategy.

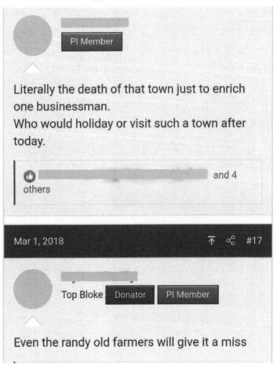

Somebody else linked the decision to the 2040 'ethnic-replacement project' [sic], meaning Ireland's National Development Plan 2040. Note the divisive use of terms like 'homogeneous' and 'non-Irish garrison' as if a foreign outpost were attacking our Irishness. The numbers are also inflated.

Interesting suggestion to get a campaign started – leaflet the town and social media. That's exactly what happened.

More misleading language: 'Obligating Lisdoonvarna permanently' in relation to a twelve-month contract.

The following post mentions a conference in London by Generation Identity Europe. This was the first official UK conference for this group of white supremacists. Generation Identity spreads the far-right conspiracy theory that white people are becoming a minority. They target teenagers and young people with a high-profile social media presence.

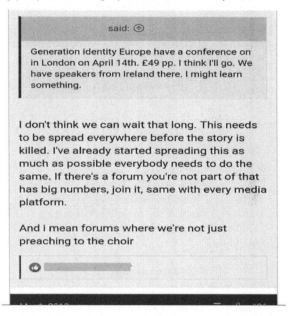

More guesswork, criticism and slander. I wonder if the posters would be ashamed if they re-read their own comments, with references to '3rd World scrounging animals' [sic] and the warning that farmers' daughters and animals need to watch out. Further down asylum seekers are referred to as aliens.

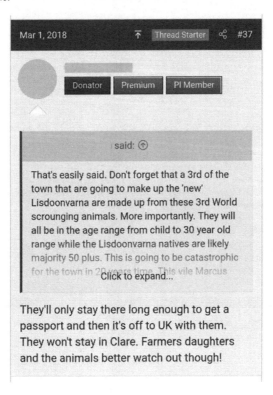

Mar 1, 2018   Thread Starter   #37

Donator   Premium   PI Member

said:

That's easily said. Don't forget that a 3rd of the town that are going to make up the 'new' Lisdoonvarna are made up from these 3rd World scrounging animals. More importantly. They will all be in the age range from child to 30 year old range while the Lisdoonvarna natives are likely majority 50 plus. This is going to be catastrophic for the town in 20 years time. This vile Marcus

Click to expand...

They'll only stay there long enough to get a passport and then it's off to UK with them. They won't stay in Clare. Farmers daughters and the animals better watch out though!

These people don't seem to see the irony of discussing Irish immigration, one having only returned to Ireland four years previously. The other thinks that we Irish are a 'nation of f*ckin small minded p*sshead clowns' [sic]. Why bother defending our culture and heritage if we're so bad?

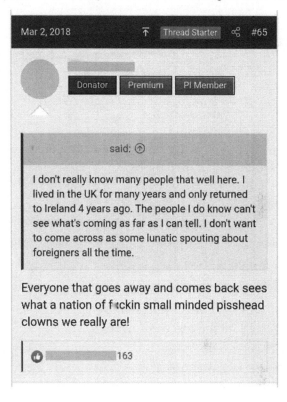

This person reckons that 'Celts are not even particularly high quality themselves' [sic]. One complaint after another. Why are these people 'protecting' us if they think our quality is questionable? Do they not realise how many Irish people have emigrated because they could not survive in their own country? Did we cause anarchy and tyranny?

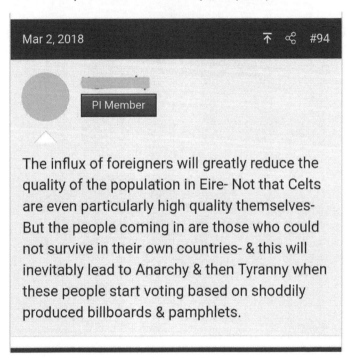

Mar 2, 2018   ⤒ ⌖ #94

PI Member

The influx of foreigners will greatly reduce the quality of the population in Eire- Not that Celts are even particularly high quality themselves- But the people coming in are those who could not survive in their own countries- & this will inevitably lead to Anarchy & then Tyranny when these people start voting based on shoddily produced billboards & pamphlets.

They appear to be discussing the 'Caring for Asylum Seekers in Lisdoonvarna' Facebook group – the one where the admins were targeted. The references, terms and words used seek to vilify, dismiss and discredit the volunteers.

Here is a reference to an echo chamber. An echo chamber evolves when like-minded people engage in conversations reaffirming each other's beliefs or facts and no longer accept facts from outside their self-af-firming sources.

Notice the divisive language again – 'destroy', 'pick out', 'target', 'conquest', 'chaos', 'globalists', 'powers that be', 'traitor'.

Yet another romantic notion of Lisdoonvarna as 'the most symbolically Irish town'.

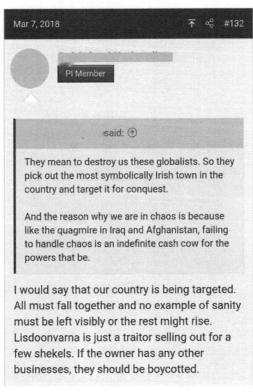

Mar 7, 2018   ⤒ ⤴ #132

PI Member

said: ⤒

They mean to destroy us these globalists. So they pick out the most symbolically Irish town in the country and target it for conquest.

And the reason why we are in chaos is because like the quagmire in Iraq and Afghanistan, failing to handle chaos is an indefinite cash cow for the powers that be.

I would say that our country is being targeted. All must fall together and no example of sanity must be left visibly or the rest might rise. Lisdoonvarna is just a traitor selling out for a few shekels. If the owner has any other businesses, they should be boycotted.

Then the *Breitbart* connection became public and a tweet linking the interview was shared on the thread. The post included the written article, which was full of romanticism and unfounded fears.

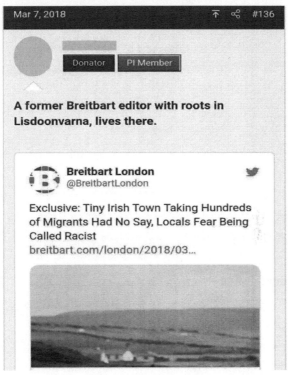

Exclusive Interview: Tiny Irish Town Taking ...

A resident of a tiny Irish town to be home to ...

breitbart.com

♡ 177   10:30 AM - Mar 7, 2018   ⓘ

💬 240 people are talking about this   ＞

Tiny Irish Town Taking Hundreds of Migrants Had No Say, Locals Fear Being Called Racist

A resident of a tiny Irish town having its population increased by a third by a new migrant centre has said Ireland has become a "slave state" of the European Union (EU) and its immigration policies, leaving locals helpless.

"We don't know where these people are going to be from. They won't tell us what countries they're from. What religion they're from," said

The interviewer and interviewee both mentioned their Irish ancestry. Do they not see the irony in being anti-immigration when they exist because of Irish people emigrating? That fact seems to be lost on so many people.

"We don't know where these people are going to be from. They won't tell us what countries they're from. What religion they're from," said ▓▓▓▓▓▓▓.

He said the 300-strong rural community of Lisdoonvarna could be radically changed by such a large and sudden influx, and that many concerned locals were fearful of accusations of racism if they questioned it.

"They just proposed to expand the population of this little village by what? Twenty-five per cent? Thirty-three per cent actually!" he exclaimed in an interview with Breitbart News Editor in Chief ▓▓▓▓▓▓ on Breitbart News Daily on Sirius XM.

Mr. ▓▓▓▓ a screenwriter, author, filmmaker, and former Breitbart News editor – grew up in the U.S. but has roots in the isolated town of Lisdoonvarna in County Clare, which hosts a popular matchmaking festival in the summer, attracting many tourists.

He returned to the area in his twenties to "reconnect" with his Irish roots and renovate a property there. Like others, he wanted to experience Irish culture and enjoy life in the traditional community, which he now fears will dramatically change.

SKIP TO 10 MINUTES:

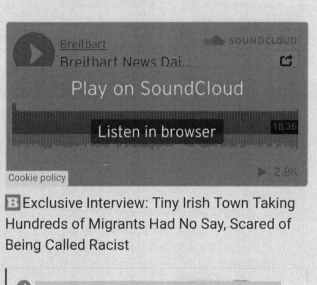

Breitbart
Breitbart News Dai...
Play on SoundCloud
Listen in browser
18:36
Cookie policy
2.8K

B Exclusive Interview: Tiny Irish Town Taking Hundreds of Migrants Had No Say, Scared of Being Called Racist

member 917

One poster believes people need to overcome their fear of being labelled racist. According to them, 'Racist is the new patriot'.

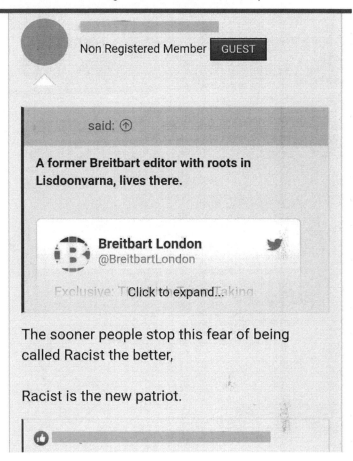

The sooner people stop this fear of being called Racist the better,

Racist is the new patriot.

There was a growing commitment that something needed to be done about immigration in Ireland. Perhaps Lisdoonvarna was a good place to start.

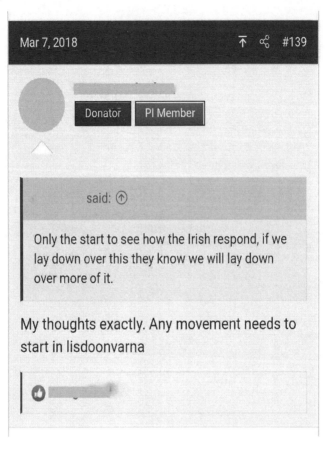

This post indicates that the National Party had no money to oppose asylum seekers in Lisdoonvarna, as the money was being spent to oppose abortion in Ireland by protecting the Eighth Amendment in the then upcoming referendum.

The National Party was very interested in Lisdoonvarna. They made a video about Lisdoonvarna that didn't include a single local person.

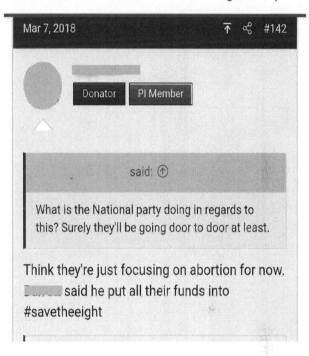

Mar 7, 2018   #142

Donator   PI Member

said: ⊕

What is the National party doing in regards to this? Surely they'll be going door to door at least.

Think they're just focusing on abortion for now. ▓▓▓▓ said he put all their funds into #savetheeight

The conversation didn't fail to demonstrate the small-mindedness of the participants.

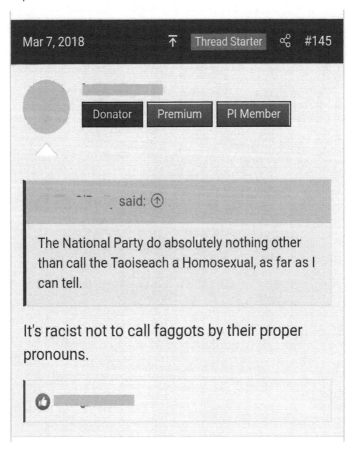

This poster picks up on the fact that wars waged by the West are creating asylum seekers.

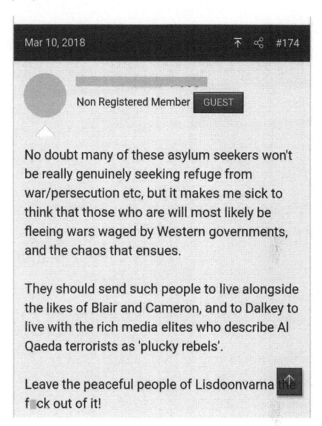

They should send such people to live alongside
Click to expand...

I completely agree. Western governments have to stop bombing the crap out of middle eastern & african countries They have no business interfering in democratically elected governments. We are now paying the price for there carnage.

We cant do anything about that. But we can and should be controlling our borders.

We need to let the sell-out ▮▮▮▮ know hes a sell-out.
Same for the hotel owner in Roscommon
There are heaps of people talking about this, and are not happy.
Once this abortion referendum is over and the repeal side destroyed, we need to turn our efforts towards project 2040 and have that dismantled.
Its clear our government dont care about the unborn or its own citizens.

Mar 10, 2018   ⌃ ⤴ #178

Pl Member

Once this abortion nonsense is over, Is it possible to turn all our attention to project 2040 and stop that also.
There are clearly a lot of people on here and elsewhere online that are against this madness. It seems there are many who are anti-abortion and anti-immigration. I dont care what other political opinion/background/thought/idea you may have, if you share those views then i will put any other difference aside and work towards putting a stop to both of the above.

The Irish people have been targeted for extermination, and its gonna happen in our lifetime. Lets do something about it before its too late

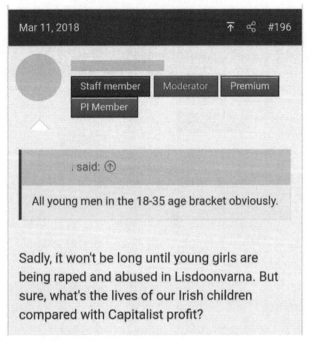

Mar 11, 2018 #196

Staff member | Moderator | Premium
PI Member

said: ⊕

All young men in the 18-35 age bracket obviously.

Sadly, it won't be long until young girls are being raped and abused in Lisdoonvarna. But sure, what's the lives of our Irish children compared with Capitalist profit?

The irony in this post is that we had to explain to the residents in Direct Provision what happens in September. We advised them to watch out for sexual predators during the matchmaking festival.

One thing we are proud of in Lisdoonvarna is that we were host to Ireland's, if not the world's, first ever LGBTQI – Lesbian, Gay, Bisexual, Transgender, Queer or Questioning, and Intersex – Matchmaking Festival. People on this site don't seem to appreciate the event as much as we do.

Mar 21, 2018   丅   ∝   #207

Shocking Stuff   Donator   PI Member

Did they have it coming I wonder the people of Lisdoonvarna?

I just googled the village name into google and this is what comes up.

Maybe its a government test case, seeing as the town is so liberal they either wanted to see how liberals coped when having scamugees dumped on them, or they wanted to see what happens when fakefugees meet Ireland's LGBT community.

Mar 21, 2018   #208

Ireland passed the Marriage Referendum in 2015, which allowed for same-sex marriage. That outcome wasn't popular in far-right circles.

Someone wonders if we had it coming to us. They question whether the government chose Lisdoonvarna because we are so liberal, so accepting of people regardless of their sexual identity.

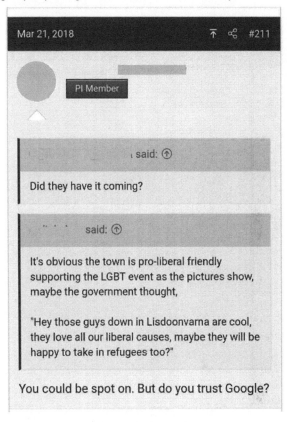

Mar 21, 2018   #211

PI Member

said: ⬆

Did they have it coming?

said: ⬆

It's obvious the town is pro-liberal friendly supporting the LGBT event as the pictures show, maybe the government thought,

"Hey those guys down in Lisdoonvarna are cool, they love all our liberal causes, maybe they will be happy to take in refugees too?"

You could be spot on. But do you trust Google?

The importance of the basic human right to dignity, equality and non-discrimination seems lost on the far right. Their attitudes towards asylum seekers, women's right to choose and sexual orientation shows their deficit of tolerance, empathy and respect.

Mar 21, 2018   ⊼ ⦷ #213

PI Member

said: ⊕

The images can be trusted.

Its obvious the town hosted an LGBT event.

Remember this is a small town in the middle of nowhere, its only claim to fame is some obscure matchmaking event.

Well, if you can impose the gay stuff, all madness can be imposed. I don't really care for the money grubbers of Lisdoonvarna. But a line must be drawn in this madness, lest we be Britain.

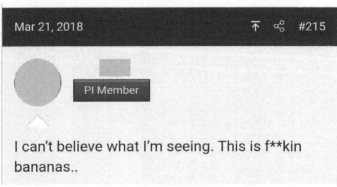

Mar 21, 2018   ⊼ ⦷ #215

PI Member

I can't believe what I'm seeing. This is f**kin bananas..

Some vital facts emerge from these conversations. The people on this forum who are so opposed to asylum seekers also oppose the major advances Ireland has made in the past few years by legalising same-sex marriage and repealing the Eighth Amendment (which made abortion illegal). These are changes that Irish citizens voted for.

There is also a regularly updated list of 'Planters'. Planters are supposedly far-left actors and government agents who support the 'Great Replacement'. I expect I was on this list.

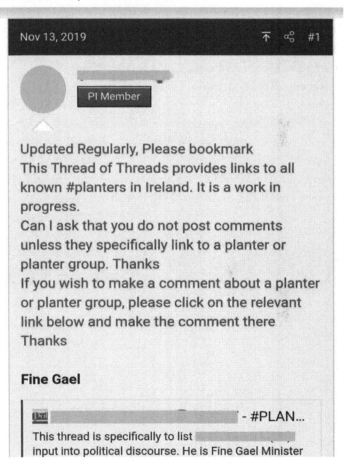

Nov 13, 2019   ⤒ ⋵ #1

PI Member

Updated Regularly, Please bookmark
This Thread of Threads provides links to all known #planters in Ireland. It is a work in progress.
Can I ask that you do not post comments unless they specifically link to a planter or planter group. Thanks
If you wish to make a comment about a planter or planter group, please click on the relevant link below and make the comment there
Thanks

Fine Gael

▒▒▒▒▒▒▒▒▒▒▒▒▒▒▒▒▒▒▒▒▒▒ - #PLAN...
This thread is specifically to list ▒▒▒▒▒▒▒▒
input into political discourse. He is Fine Gael Minister

This is a snapshot. There is no way of knowing who is being influenced by these articles or how they react. All of this contributes to a rise in the number of people thinking in this way as they gravitate towards the echo chambers of these forums. They are immersed in these messages.

There is no doubt that the internet plays a big role in movements for political, social and environmental change. Social media can facilitate the rapid growth and spread of information. However, one big problem with online communication and sharing is that fake news, bigotry and incitement to hate can be left unchecked, considered fact and spread across the world within seconds. A racist chat room inciting hate and anger rubs off on people in that room as they relate to and trust each other. This is a worrying trend and seems to be driving division within society.

In January 2023 a group of homeless migrants living in tents were attacked by a violent mob with dogs, using baseball bats and batons. Another incident saw verbal and physical abuse of healthcare workers where one nurse was threatened with stabbing. A nurse! These incidents happened while lies attributing rapes, violence and attacks to asylum seekers and refugees were flooding social media. This is way out of hand and existing laws must be implemented to stop it.

> Truly, whoever can make you believe absurdities can make you commit atrocities.
>
> Voltaire

5

Familiar Strangers

The asylum seekers who arrived in Lisdoonvarna were acutely aware of the No vote and local objections to Direct Provision. Many were fearful about moving to a community they perceived as hostile. Through the Caring for Asylum Seekers group, people worked together to host a welcome event. Residents from all over North Clare came with baked goods, savoury foods and refreshments to welcome our new residents. Musicians from across the county came along to get the party going. It was very satisfying to finally watch the asylum seekers mingling with people from the area. We had accomplished something, despite all of the negativity and abuse. The *Céad Míle Fáilte* was alive and well. In the Irish language this means one hundred thousand welcomes.

One memory I will hold dear from that day was meeting Mansoureh. She had travelled from Iran, where six of her siblings were killed for their activism. They were killed by the Iranian government, an Islamist theocracy that tends to function like a dictatorship. Mansoureh is a human rights and women's rights activist seeking truth and justice. She walked up to me as I was serving tea and asked whom she should talk to about activism in the area. I was delighted to tell her that she had come to the right person!

I soon found myself sitting down over a cup of tea, chatting with an activist just like me. Unlike me, she carries the pain and loss of her loved ones paying the ultimate price for justice. She had to flee her home because of her quest for truth and justice. I felt very privileged and proud that I played a very small part in helping Mansoureh. That day, at our welcome reception, I knew I had done the right thing. She went on to collaborate with the Clare branch of the Women's Collective Ireland, a feminist network based in Clare, to inspire others and speak at events, as have other women from the centre.

Following the death in police custody of 22-year-old Mahsa (Jina) Amini on 16 September 2022 in Iran, Mansoureh and other Iranian activists have been involved actively in Ireland, in solidarity with the protesters of Iran in the uprising of 'woman, life, freedom'. There have been major civil struggles in Iran since Mahsa's murder, with ongoing civil rights violations, killing and arresting protesters, as well as internet and social media blackouts by the Iranian regime.

Many Iranians outside Iran, as well as citizens, activists and feminists from all over the world, have been supporting this movement of the Iranian people, especially the brave women of Iran for their fight to end and resistance to discrimination and dictatorship in Iran. Some countries have also imposed sanctions in response to the Iranian regime's suppression. Mansoureh is still seeking truth and justice. For more information you can follow the activities of this group – called SEFI, 'Support Equality & Freedom for Iran' – a politically independent group of Irish-Iranian and Iranian professionals. You can follow 'Sefi_ireland' and 'IrishIranians' on Instagram or Twitter.

The residents of the Direct Provision centre were mostly women and children. Within a few months of the centre opening in Lisdoonvarna, Ireland voted on a change to our Constitution. This referendum was commonly referred to as 'Repeal the Eighth', 'Right to Choose' or 'the abortion referendum'. We were voting on a woman's right to choose to terminate her pregnancy in Ireland under certain conditions. An article in the Constitution had to be repealed to allow this to happen. A lot of the conversations over tea in the first few months were about women's rights

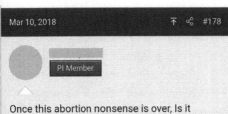

PI Member

Once this abortion nonsense is over, Is it possible to turn all our attention to project 2040 and stop that also.
There are clearly a lot of people on here and elsewhere online that are against this madness. It seems there are many who are anti-abortion and anti-immigration. I dont care what other political opinion/background/thought/idea you may have, if you share those views then i will put any other difference aside and work towards putting a stop to both of the above.

The Irish people have been targeted for extermination, and its gonna happen in our lifetime. Lets do something about it before its too late

and abortion. As we got to know each other online and in person we often discussed this national conversation.

Of course, not everyone opposed to abortion is from the far-right or opposed to asylum seekers. However, opposition to abortion and immigration are part of far-right ideology. This can be seen in the policies of far-right political parties and on the screen-shots in the previous chapter.

This poster anticipated that the campaign against abortion would win the referendum and that they could then turn their attention to dismantling Project Ireland 2040 – the supposed 'ethnic-replacement project' or, as per the *Breitbart* article 'policy to dramatically grow the nation's population through mass migration.' This person seriously believed that 'the Irish people have been targeted for extermination.'

If you were around Lisdoonvarna in the run-up to the referendum you would probably have expected overwhelming local opposition to changing the Constitution. There were massive billboards outside both Lisdoonvarna and Doolin churches. There were No posters everywhere. There was an active No campaign in the area, both physically and online.

In contrast the couple of Yes posters in the village looked as though they had been planted by someone passing through while everyone slept.

In spite of this, we joined the rest of Ireland in a landslide Yes vote on Friday 25 May, 2018. Almost 70% of those who voted in Lisdoonvarna chose Yes. Nearby, Doolin voted 75% Yes. Nationally, at just over 64%, voter turnout for the referendum was the highest since the first Referendum

Commission was established in 1998. A Yes majority had been expected in urban areas but nobody predicted the massive support it had in rural Ireland.

There had been a major online campaign called 'In Her Shoes'. Personal stories were submitted, accompanied by a photograph of shoes, to share with the world, anonymously on social media. The depth and detail of the stories shared demonstrated how many people in Ireland were affected by the issues and subsequently empowered to help change Irish society. There were heart-wrenching stories from people with experiences of problematic pregnancies, stillbirths, miscarriages, institutional abuse, abortion, rape and much more. These stories have since been published in a book titled *In Her Shoes*.

Our national broadcaster, RTÉ, reported that 43% of voters were influenced by personal stories covered in the media and 34% were influenced by personal stories from people they knew. Social media had played a massive role in the referendum, as had been anticipated early on. Just as it had when Direct Provision was proposed for Lisdoonvarna.

I see a lot of similarities between what happened in response to the proposed Direct Provision centre in Lisdoonvarna and the referendum three months later. The silent majority remained anonymous, which meant that those who were vocal projected a very different impression of the true opinions of the community. Those who were the most vocal and aggressive during the referendum campaign turned out to be in the minority. However, there were a few people in the Lisdoonvarna area who were openly supportive of a Yes vote. We were challenged online for our opinion, even while sharing the true accounts of people's lives.

Things developed similarly with Direct Provision. There was a small group of aggressive online objectors who attacked anyone who seemed sympathetic to refugees or asylum seekers coming to Lisdoonvarna. If someone questioned the credibility or reliability of videos claiming to depict asylum seekers, refugees or immigrants running riot elsewhere, they were immediately discredited, challenged and dismissed. The same videos are still being used to recruit support.

In Lisdoonvarna there was definitely a silent majority who kept quiet during the referendum campaign but voiced their opinion when they came out to vote. There were also many people waiting in the wings who wanted to help asylum seekers. In my role as a change-maker and activist I have become increasingly aware of this silent body of people.

> All tyranny needs to gain a foothold is for people of good conscience to remain silent.
>
> Thomas Jefferson

I believe that we need many more people confident enough to speak up. We need that silent majority to break the mould and be more vocal earlier on. We need them to overcome the debilitating fear of speaking up and being judged. We need them to stop worrying so much about what their neighbours think.

An Ironic Twist

One of the most inspirational and moving aspects of voting day was the #hometovote phenomenon. Thousands of people travelled back to Ireland to vote. There were pictures and news reports from airports and seaports showing determined, mostly young, faces coming home to vote.

These were Irish people coming home from abroad to vote because Irish citizens can't vote from abroad with a postal vote. They made the long journey home because they cared so much that Ireland's Constitution and laws would reflect their values. I expect many plan to come home to settle in the future. Videos from the airport of groups of young people in Repeal jumpers arriving home to vote were very emotive. I was so proud that they cared enough to exercise their right to vote.

Ironically, these were Irish people living and working abroad. Irish people spread all over the world. I wonder were they made welcome wherever they had moved to live and work or study?

The Rise of Caring

My first visit to the Direct Provision centre was for an Irish music event for St Patrick's Day in March 2018. A small group went to the centre on

Rubber Bandits ✔
@Rubberbandits

Looking forward to Christmas in the pub where I can hear ould lads complaining about immigration while simultaneously bragging about how much their son is earning in Australia

19:30 · 13 Nov 19 · Twitter for iPhone

the morning of St Patrick's Day with some green, white and orange items including hats and flags. We brought face paints to draw shamrocks and Irish flags on peoples faces. This would be the first community event the asylum seekers would attend in Lisdoonvarna and we wanted it to be welcoming. We aimed to help everyone feel included, to be part of our national celebration in some small way.

I remember thinking how small the lobby of the building was, given that it was the main communal space. It was early days and there were only 30 residents, sitting with a group of about ten locals. Most of the chairs and sofas were occupied. The number of residents was set to increase dramatically and it didn't look big enough to accommodate 115 people comfortably. The play area was an open-plan room just off the communal space. There was no escape from the noise of the children and the toys. It all seemed very cramped, and with three times as many people expected, I wondered how they would live together, all under the same roof.

It was then that I realised how important it would be to organise some-where outside of the centre for people to go. That was one insight that stood out for me when we had discussed Direct Provision with those working with asylum seekers – how difficult school holidays are for families stuck in one bedroom. Now, having seen the inside of the building that our new neighbours would call 'home', I felt compelled to ensure that they could get out of it as much as they needed to.

I've been working in sustainable community development for many years. My favourite projects are community gardens, allotments, Tidy Towns, men's sheds, and skills workshops. Basically anything that includes environmental protection and skill-sharing while bringing people together with a cup of tea. I had also coordinated one of Dublin's largest summer camps many years ago and reckoned that we could try something like that in Lisdoonvarna.

There was no shortage of like-minded people. With the help of Clare PPN we organised some workshops with volunteers who wanted to become involved with asylum seekers. About ten people came forward to form a core group. We had to evaluate the need for, and merits of, establishing a brand-new group to work on integration or to piggyback onto an existing group. We came up with a mission statement and some aims we all felt strongly about. We held media training so that members would be able to deal with the continued media attention. This all helped us to get to know each other better.

On 20 April, 2018 the group LINKS – Lisdoonvarna Is Nurturing Knowledge & Solidarity was launched.

The workshops had helped figure out its direction and purpose. The group introduction states:

> When a group of us working on welcoming asylum seekers to Lisdoonvarna met to consider a future pathway, our shared, overpowering commitment was that whatever we do, it is for everyone. When we hold coffee mornings, they will be for everyone to attend. When we start a community garden, it is for everyone. When we host celebrations, they are cele-brations for the whole community. Obviously helping the asylum seekers has started this process and we felt bringing our actions out of the hotel and into the community was more beneficial for everyone. LINKS is community development

addressing rural isolation, loneliness and integration through social activities, skill-sharing and learning.

LISDOONVARNA
Nurturing Knowledge & Solidarity

BUILDING BRIDGES ACROSS OUR COMMUNITY

Join us for a cuppa

Where? In the Pavilion
When? Thursday May 24
Time? 10.30am to 12pm

Everyone is welcome and we ask you to let others know especially anyone living alone or in need of a little company.

Having organised a welcome gathering, LINKS had to set about fund-raising so that they could organise community events to encourage people to get out and get together. Community events offer a space outside of the centre for residents but require insurance, rent and refreshments, at the very least. What struck me as extremely lacking was the failure of RIA to support the local community that rallies around to help. In Lisdoonvarna a group formed very quickly but was not supported financially by RIA. If an existing group has the capacity and resources to fill the role of host then that is great, but many don't.

From the start, volunteers organised regular coffee mornings, drama, dance and many arts and craft activities. These events encouraged integration by providing opportunities for the entire community to gather together outside of the centre. Local businesses paid for buses to bring the residents on day trips to various activities provided free of charge by other local businesses, including swimming, ferry trips, yoga and surfing. A branch of Fáilte Isteach was established. Fáilte Isteach is a community project that involves volunteers welcoming migrants through conversational English classes. As with many positions, people volunteered and had to be Garda-vetted and trained. It was a serious commitment.

Cynthia, a local crafter, received support from Clare Local Development Company to organise a craft class every week. She was joined by other crafters, seamstresses and artists. Residents had the opportunity to sew, make jewellery and participate in other creative activities. People donated sewing machines. There was an ebb and flow of participants as they began receiving language classes, work permits and having other vital integration needs met. These volunteers were also welcomed at the centre, as some women were afraid to leave the centre alone due to past trauma or were too shy due to the language barrier.

The volunteers were pleased to offer some of the women the opportunity to teach and share their skills. The organisers set up a market to enable those with work permits to sell their wares. It was a great success, as the locals wanted to support the asylum seekers but were not sure what they could do. The market ran until summer jobs began, the families involved got their papers and left the centre or were relocated to other centres around the country.

Performing arts proved to be extremely powerful for integration. Marcella, a human rights advocate and choreographer living in Clare, offered to help and so began an eighteen-month journey. Her initial project was a children's talent camp and show called 'Lisdoonvarna's Got Talent'. It ran during the 2018 summer holidays and gave all children in the area an opportunity to mingle ahead of the start of the school year.

At the grand finale participants got to show their individual talents and perform acts they had worked on. The last act was a song through Irish sign language, a new language they all learned together during the camp. The show was a great celebration of community and parents attended the end of camp party.

Over the course of a few months of participating in coffee mornings, creative activities, referendum discussions and summer camps, it became very clear that the women in Direct Provision had many stories, a lot of talent and wanted to be involved in the community. Marcella also worked on a project for Heritage Week. The theme for 2018 was 'Sharing a Story' and she worked with some local women to write a play. They shared their stories and experiences with institutions charged with caring for women and children. She invited the women from Direct Provision to join the cast.

The similar experiences and shared stories of the women in Direct Provision and Irish women were striking. Our stories were intertwined and the show told the tales of many inequalities and women's resilience. It involved four generations and we explored how Ireland would look in 2050.

A couple of asylum seekers told a story of how unmarried pregnant women were taken to the jungle to starve, be killed by wild animals or thrown to their death from a cliff. A decision was made by the village in which the women's parents had no say. If they tried to interfere the mother would also be punished.

Irish women told stories of life in Ireland's laundries and Mother and Baby Homes. One had been pregnant and unmarried as a girl and the other had been adopted as a baby. These institutions operated in Ireland until 1996 and were mostly run by religious organisations. Pregnant women and their children worked for their keep. Most of the babies were conceived outside of marriage.

Mansoureh also told the story of what happened to her in Iran. After the 1979 Revolution, all opposition parties, trade unions, women's and student groups and even professional organisations, the bar, and writers became victims of massive, organised attacks and tens of thousands disappeared.

She was imprisoned in Mashad for 100 days in 1981 when she was six months pregnant. A week before her daughter was born she was released on bail due to much petitioning from her family. She, along with her husband and daughter, lived in secret for several years, afraid to be seen in public places. After the great prison massacre of 1988, the first of many mass graves was found. She lost her older sister, four brothers and her brother-in-law in the massacres of the 1980s.

Several other poets, musicians and dancers performed. I read poems about my grandad and ancestral village, Gleninagh, which is now a shell of its former self as generations have emigrated.

The show was a tapestry of music, poetry, song, storytelling, sign language and dance, looking back on old Ireland and integrating the new Ireland. Now that these women were safe in Ireland the show gave the women in Direct Provision an opportunity to express the trauma that they had experienced. Emigration and immigration were very much a part of the show. So many people from Ireland left here and as we welcome asylum seekers it's an opportunity for us to be generous in return. Even though our language was different we discovered in the show that we all had relatable stories, one voice and a shared vision for a better world.

Marcella's next project was 'You think you can dance', a charity fundraiser for children with disabilities. The concept was to teach adults in the wider community a new skill but to also give them an understanding of how difficult it is for someone with a disability to learn and grow without continuous support. The women from Direct Provision did a traditional dance on the night and won the audience over, taking home a trophy. Despite where they were living, they still wanted to be part of their community by giving their time, talent and empathy to support the charity night.

Finally, Marcella crafted a show of gratitude in 2019. With all of their talent and confidence, the women and children who found themselves in Direct Provision wanted to thank Lisdoonvarna for welcoming them with a performance and by sharing their national dishes. Hands in Harmony, a deaf choir from neighbouring County Limerick, were guest artists on the day. Once again the performance made it very clear that everyone stood as one voice to achieve the same outcome. Everyone on stage was equal, regardless of race, culture, religion, language, disability or gender.

In the early months we shared and discussed many life stories in which the oppression of women and the vulnerable was a common theme. Many stories related to the rejection, shaming and institutionalisation of women and children. Pregnancy was a common reason for cruelty and injustice. In Ireland, many babies were taken from or abandoned by their shamed mothers. Even though the state paid for their care, many were neglected and died. As well as being paid by the state, the religious orders made money by working the women in their laundries, selling babies to adoptive parents, conducting vaccine trials and selling corpses as anatomical subjects for medical research. These institutions are now closed.

During the referendum to Repeal the Eighth, about 77% of voters were influenced by personal stories in the media or from people they knew. It's reasonable to believe that the large Yes vote in rural Ireland was in part influenced by so many people who knew what had happened inside the state- and church-run institutions located throughout the country. The horror stories that they had heard had taken place in those daunting buildings that were part of their communities have been proven true.

Ireland has a shameful history of turning a blind eye to profiteering, as pregnancy, childbirth, disability, orphans, abandoned children and vulnerable adults provided guaranteed income to service providers. The same is true for asylum seekers, the homeless and many vulnerable people today. It's said that the character of a community can be judged by how they treat their most vulnerable. In Ireland the care, or supposed care, of the vulnerable can be a very lucrative business. The more corners you cut, the greater the profits. Over the course of working on the show we came to recognise Direct Provision as Ireland's new laundries. The sharing of stories between asylum seekers and survivors of institutional abuse created connection, appreciation and mutual understanding.

The attitudes within the Irish state and Church that enabled them to feel justified and entitled to incarcerate women and children in this way are not something that simply disappears when the gates of an old building are locked. There is definitely a certain amount of shame attached to this chapter of Ireland's history, but also a lot of defensiveness and reluctance to dismantle the system that facilitated it. One church is still connected to education, health care and the media. It is still supported by society and communities, filling social, cultural and spiritual needs.

There is still nothing being done to prevent and reverse the profit-driven care model. Landlords and service providers are still receiving millions of euros of taxpayers' money to 'care' for the vulnerable.

Covid-19 has also shown us that the neglect of the vulnerable by the system continues. More than half of all deaths – almost 1,000 – in the first four months of the pandemic were in nursing homes. This trend was repeated in subsequent waves of infection. Covid-19 also spread through numerous Direct Provision centres. We cannot trust the state to care for the vulnerable in our society and it is good to see people holding the government to account on their behalf when it happens.

LINKS have gone on to organise many get-togethers, summer projects, seasonal parties and activities for adults and children. During Covid-19 they were involved in projects to create Halloween, Christmas and celebratory spectacles in the park to support wellbeing and socially distanced community engagement.

I believe that having this structured approach from early on has ensured that the management of the centre knows that the community in Lisdoonvarna cares about the residents. Members of LINKS are welcome to engage with residents in the centre, at residents' invitation. They are also invited to events and stakeholder meetings. They liaise with Clare Immigration Support Centre and with the Clare branch of the Women's Collective Ireland. I believe that the members of LINKS have done an absolutely amazing job. Their existence ensures that the residents feel supported and that the centre management feel accountable. They have been and continue to be the backbone of our community response.

In a survey I conducted in 2019, I asked if people had had any interaction with residents of the centre and to share their experiences. The feedback was very positive. Many people had met residents at community events organised by LINKS. Three respondents had worked with or employed residents and had great praise for their work and social interactions. One response I must quote covers a lot of the sentiment: 'We should feel honoured to know and help these people. They have helped develop my family, my understanding and the community. I feel embarrassed that I did not understand more about this and welcome these families straight away. I'm annoyed at the lies and the underhanded government approach.'

People can be amazing. The time, effort, solidarity, resilience and mutual support of volunteers within Lisdoonvarna maintained my faith in humanity. There were some pretty nasty episodes early on, but the people who rose to the challenge and continue to welcome and care for asylum seekers in Lisdoonvarna are a gift to our society.

It also taught me that we have a real problem with social and rural isolation. By hosting events for asylum seekers and inviting everyone, we met people who rarely engaged socially with anyone outside of their home. There were some people living locally who really looked forward to the gatherings. This was part of the vision for LINKS and it has been great to see it happen.

Volunteers are the backbone of Irish society and Lisdoonvarna is alive with volunteers across many areas, including sports, youth activities, the environment, the arts, caregiving, fundraising, community development and more. I'd say at this stage all of the volunteers and more have helped asylum seekers get involved in activities in Lisdoonvarna.

Of course, volunteers let the state off the hook, big time. I wonder if RIA could walk away from a community if volunteers didn't step up? How should RIA support people within host communities who come forward? These are fundamental questions that need to be asked for whatever systems are put in place for asylum seekers and other vulnerable members of our society. Following rebranding, the RIA is now known as the International Protection Accommodation Services (IPAS).

> The greatness of a community is most accurately measured by the compassionate actions of its members.
>
> Coretta Scott King

6

Changing Ireland

Covid-19 has demonstrated how quickly Ireland and the world can change when the need and political will are there. The following issues, while independent, they intersect. We need to change the system to address them, once and for all.

Homelessness

Mansoureh was the first asylum seeker I knew personally who was granted refugee status. Then she had to find a home, a job and face all the challenges that came with her 'freedom'. Since then, others have moved on. When some of the children left during the Covid-19 lockdown, we held a drive-through so that their classmates could wave goodbye.

Many people cite housing our own homeless before asylum seekers as a reason to oppose Direct Provision. There is a housing crisis in Ireland but being hostile towards asylum seekers and refugees is not the way to change government policy. Successive governments have failed to build adequate social or affordable housing. Local authorities saw no reason to build social housing during the Celtic Tiger boom years. The government back then anticipated that almost everyone would be able to afford their own home and requested that developers include social housing in their developments for those who couldn't buy. That didn't work. Then we bailed out the banks when the economy crashed. Those same banks have been repossessing homes ever since and vulture funds are permitted to buy them for a pittance. This is government policy favouring the financial institutions, supporting privatisation and the capitalisation, or profit-driven supply, of basic needs. The neoliberal norm for the twenty-first century.

In December 2022, 1,594 families, with 3,442 children, in Ireland were homeless according to the Department of Housing, Planning & Local Government Homelessness Report. A total of 8,190 adults were homeless. On 1 January 2023 there were 19,104 people in Direct Provision, including 3,928 children.

The official homelessness data published by the Department of Housing identifies the number of people using state-funded emergency homeless accommodation. The official figures do not include those who are in 'own-door' or self-contained temporary accommodation, domestic violence refuges, asylum seekers, or people who are sleeping rough. They don't include the 'hidden homeless' staying with family or friends in insecure housing either.

The mental health impacts of becoming homeless are difficult to imagine. Stress, depression, trauma, anxiety, devastation, helplessness and more. It also impacts children. We are raising a generation of children scarred by the challenges associated with homelessness. Focus Ireland commissioned research on the impact of homelessness on families and children and the following insightful summary is from the September 2017 report by Dr Kathy Walsh and Brian Harvey, entitled 'Finding a Home: Families' Journeys out of Homelessness'.

> The experience of homelessness was cumulatively greatly distressing: in the first instance, a short period of high-intensity stress and panic, followed by prolonged stress of less intensity. Being homeless puts enormous stress on the relationship

between parents, both those living together and those living apart, and on relationships with their children.

The impacts of the experience of homelessness varied. For very young children, it appeared – from the perspective of their parents – to have had limited impact. These young children appeared largely unaware of the nature or significance of the experience. For older children, the impact was greater and more visible. For the parent/s, it was a time of considerable stress, intensive at first, then of less intensity, but prolonged and just as potentially scarring, often resulting in significant friction between parents. Personal relationships and family discipline generally deteriorated.

Among the principal problems were the lack of certainty, lack of play space, poor conditions in some locations, over-crowding, boredom and reduced socialisation. Specific impacts on parents were noted as food-related (weight gain/ weight loss, deterioration in health), emotional (loss of confidence) and economic (loss of employment, the cost of eating out, spending of any savings). Many families lost all of their possessions, bar what they could carry, and this was a cause of emotional distress for some families.

Although some emergency accommodation was of good quality, some was poor, characterised by overcrowding of washing and bathroom facilities and limited/no access to cooking facilities. Getting children to school and keeping them attending their existing schools were also key pressure points. Transport was a particular issue, with families with cars having an advantage in being able to transport their children across town more efficiently and having a location where they could wait until school was over. For those dependent on buses, this process took much longer and was much more physically tiring and ultimately more stressful.

Local authorities were identified as having a crucial role to play as the provider of both emergency and longer-term accommodation, as well as the administrator of the HAP (Housing Assistance Payment) scheme. The families raised concerns both about the ability of the local authorities to meet growing needs and about the manner in which some local authorities transacted their business, from their apparent lack of engagement in any form of prevention, to the poor treatment of clients by a small number of local authority personnel.

We need strong social housing policy and government commitment to provide affordable housing for everyone who requires it. We do not need to be spending millions on emergency accommodation and Direct Provision, giving money to landlords and profiteers. Wasn't that what happened when we were oppressed by the British? That money could be used to build and maintain homes as national assets.

Perhaps we could introduce a land value tax to deter land hoarders from preventing the development of homes. Or tax landlords out of the market. That would, in turn, drive down property prices, which are currently determined by those who claim ownership to more than their fair share.

There are lots of vacant properties and publicly owned land, so more can and must be done about homelessness. We need housing owned by the taxpayer, built on that public land and managed by a public housing authority. Somewhere for people in need of a home to stay until they can get onto their feet. This would provide local employment both at the building or refurbishing stage and through ongoing maintenance. If it didn't work previously then it's time to try a different way. To think outside the box.

The Covid-19 pandemic has forced changes to ensure that those classified as homeless have somewhere to stay. Despite these temporary measures, people are still dying on our streets. We need long-term, adequate, sustainable solutions.

Ireland as a US Military 'Cooperative Security Location'

Why are asylum seekers migrating in the first place? Many have to leave their homes because of war. During 2020 America was involved in wars with Syria, Afghanistan and Somalia. These are three of the top five countries of origin for refugees. US army planes routinely stop in Shannon and refuel before flying to war zones further east.

The group Shannonwatch is 'an initiative of peace and human rights activists to document the use of Shannon airport by the United States of America for the purposes of waging war and committing human rights abuse'. It was established to 'end US military use of Shannon airport, to stop rendition flights through the airport, and to obtain accountability for both from the relevant Irish authorities and political leaders'. They meet for a peaceful protest at Shannon airport on the second Sunday of each month, usually at 2 p.m. You can find more information online.

I wonder how many American military planes using Shannon airport contribute to migration.

Racism and Hate Crime

'Direct Division' is a 2020 report by the Ombudsman for Children's Office that highlights the views and experiences of children living in Direct Provision. The report explores the children's lives in Direct Provision accommodation, as well as their experiences of inclusion and exclusion at school, in the local community and wider Irish society. To highlight the heart-breaking contents of the report, here is an excerpt:

> Exclusion in School
> Many of the participants talked about feeling excluded in school. For some children getting to and from school contributed to their sense of exclusion, as they travelled to school together on buses that only served the accommodation centre. This marked them out as being from the Direct Provision centre

when they arrived at and left school and as being different to their peers.

Many of the children that we spoke to described incidents of bullying, racism and discrimination while in school, all of which made them feel excluded from normal school life. They explained that both their peers and their teachers contributed to this exclusion. This exclusion ranged from not being selected by their peers and teachers for activities such as sports teams, presentations or projects, to serious allegations of racial abuse. These incidents are affecting the children's ability to fully partic-ipate in school life; with some children explaining that they do not participate in class because their peers will not work with them and others explaining that their exclusion means they will not speak or answer questions in class. The following depicts these issues.

'The first attitude they give you when you go to school it's weird, they don't see you like a normal person but when the Spanish exchange student comes it's normal, they're white... They do the 'us and them' system. Like most of the time you see black people talking on their own and the white people on their own, it's like separate, like people don't like to mix in school. Or you are in a group and you just see one black person stand in the corner. They are not open to come and start a conversation with you. They feel like you are going to bite them or something. I would tell them that words hurt, words can kill and they should watch what they say about people.'

Participant 1: '... when the teacher says "get into pairs" you're always the one left behind if your friend isn't there... you're always the last one... They don't ever like say, come with us. So the teacher is like, "it's okay, you can come with me"... all the time, every time'.

Participant 2: 'I like going to school, but then you know, sometimes when you have like a challenge, you're kind of like, "oh no" ... there are classes that you'd have with your friends that you really like but there are certain classes that if you're not friendly with a lot of the kids in there, you just like kind of dread walking in... you just want the class to finish'.

Participant 3: 'Half of my friends have moved, so I'm always like in a class on my own. So, like I dread going into some classes, but I just sit there and just do nothing all the time'.

Use of racist remarks was reported by every group of children we engaged with and was commonly cited as a source of exclusion in school. Children had experienced being called racist names such as 'Black monkey' and 'a chocolate'. A number of participants talked about the use of the 'N' word by their peers in school and to those who asked if they could use the 'N' word.

'There is this group of guys in school who come up and ask for the "N" word pass, because the "N" word seems cool. It is in rap videos. It doesn't seem right for a white person to be using that word, so I just said no... Sometimes even your friends ask, maybe they don't know it is offensive so they might ask in a jokey way... It makes me disappointed. It is not necessary; I'm in school to learn my stuff. If someone asks me that, it makes me feel uncomfortable.'

Bullying was related to race, religion and nationality. Social media was also frequently used to engage in such bullying.

'On Snapchat – 'black + tree = monkey; all African people drink dirty water; and I wouldn't go out with a black girl'.

Religion and religious expression was also cited as a reason children believed that they were being bullied. One girl explained that her religious and cultural expression through wearing the hijab made her feel unsafe. She told us that when her family first moved to Ireland her father believed that it was unsafe for her and her sister to wear their head scarves to school.

'People are racist here and there are many attacks and stuff so it's better to go with the flow and not wear the headscarf...it was sad and my mom was against it [removing the hijab]. She was like 'you just have to believe in yourself and God' but my Dad was like 'it's for safety.'

Other girls told us that their schools had banned the wearing of the head scarf citing health and safety or a uniform code as the reasoning behind this decision. This led to some girls having to remove their head scarves at the school gates or opting for other schools that allowed it.

Religion, and particularly being of the Muslim faith, was often cited as a source of bullying and exclusion, with one girl explaining:

'... Racism is regarding refugees and immigrants that's it and if you're Muslim as well, that big racism here. "Oh you're a Muslim, so are you a terrorist as well? Do you have a bomb?" Just because we are Muslim doesn't mean we are terrorists or anything. There is loads of racism in this society.'

Covert racism was often described by boys whose peers and teachers relied on common stereotypes to engage them in conversation.

'If someone looks at me, the first thing they think of is "he's black", so they start talking about basketball or hip hop.'

One girl summed up this feeling of subtle forms of racism and exclusion by stating:

'They don't exclude you; you know exclude; I mean they just don't include you'.

Many of the participants believed that if teachers and Irish children were made aware of human and children's rights and the impact of racism that they would treat asylum seekers better.

The consultation was undertaken between June and November 2019, involving 73 children aged between 12 and 17 in nine Direct Provision centres around Ireland. The report is available online and has many messages of hope and gratitude to the Irish people.

In October 2019, a mixed-race couple living in Ireland who appeared in an advertisement campaign for a major supermarket chain decided to leave Ireland after being subjected to online abuse and receiving a death threat. The following was a tweet sent on 7 September 2019 by an Irish former journalist who had previously run a campaign to seek office as the President of Ireland and who continues to seek public representative positions as a far-right candidate.

> German dump @****_ireland gaslighting the Irish people with their multicultural version of 'The Ryans'. Kidding no-one! Resist the Great Replacement wherever you can by giving this kip a wide berth. #ShopIrish #BuyIrish.

Nine months later Twitter permanently suspended the former journalist's account for 'repeated violations of the Twitter rules'. These included violations of its abusive behaviour and sensitive media policies. In 2022 her account was reinstated.

This person continues to incite people to hate others under the guise of free speech and is one of many people in Irish politics who are tolerated despite their racism. Some of these people were involved in the online campaign against Lisdoonvarna and other proposed Direct Provision centres since then.

These people are given access to the population of Ireland and the world by being welcomed on most mass media platforms. Our national broadcaster has had known racists on, possibly as a strategy to increase viewer numbers. This has the potential to increase incidences of racism and actions such as those that resulted in the couple fleeing the country, arson attacks on proposed Direct Provision sites and threats towards elected representatives. There is a link between hate speech and racially motivated attacks – it normalises racism and allows people to feel that it's acceptable to go further. It serves to build momentum for the far-right agenda.

It is accepted that a hate crime is an offence that is committed in a context that includes hostility towards difference. Up until 2020 Ireland remained one of a small number of EU countries without specific laws to deal with hate crimes.

One of the residents in Direct Provision that I was chatting with at the Clare Women's Network Silence+Voice, A Festival of Feminisms event in 2019 mentioned the racism she witnessed towards a Traveller.

I'll expand on that – I heard from an asylum seeker how she was appalled by the way a Traveller was treated by an Irish person at work. Earlier, I referred to the ECRI, which specialises in questions relating to racism and intolerance. It has welcomed some positive developments in Ireland but some issues have given rise to concern. I listed some issues but excluded the following.

Discrimination cases involving licensed premises can still only be heard by District Courts, which may be a barrier to access to justice for members of the Traveller community. Civil legal aid is not available for proceedings before the Workplace Relations Commission and the name of this body could be misleading.

The majority of local authorities have consistently failed to provide adequate and culturally appropriate accommodation for Travellers. The National Traveller and Roma Inclusion Strategy contains no actions related to accommodation for Roma. The current housing crisis with severe shortages, high rent prices and discrimination against migrants creates enormous challenges for vulnerable communities.

Thankfully, a comprehensive list of measures is available to deal with hate crimes. In its 2019 report on Ireland, ECRI requests that the authorities act in a number of areas. It makes a series of recommendations that the people of Ireland must demand. We must insist that the government act immediately to implement these recommendations, which include the following:

- New hate speech and hate crime legislation should be enacted in consultation with relevant civil society actors.
- An improved mechanism for collecting disaggregated data on hate crimes, including hate speech, should be established.
- Data regarding the motive behind the hate crime that is invoked at all stages of the investigation, prosecution, conviction and sentencing should be recorded systematically and made available to the public.
- Alternative mechanisms should be set up to encourage victims to report hate crime incidents, such as third-party reporting systems or dedicated telephone lines, in cooperation with relevant NGOs.
- Ethnic profiling by the police should be clearly defined and prohibited by law.
- All police should be thoroughly trained in identifying, recording and investigating hate crimes.
- More Ethnic Liaison Officers and LGBT Liaison Officers should be recruited and trained and diversity in the police should be increased.
- The Employment Equality Acts and the Equal Status Acts should be amended to explicitly include the ground of gender identity.
- A new and updated strategy against racism should be developed, with a strong focus on reducing prejudice against the most vulnerable and targeted communities, including Travellers, Roma, migrants and Muslims.
- Efforts to meet the accommodation needs of Travellers should be increased, including by improving existing halting sites to meet decent and safe living standards, and by providing adequate, accessible, suitable and culturally appropriate accommodation.
- A solution should be found to the issue of local authorities' failure to use funding allocated for Traveller accommodation, by imposing dissuasive sanctions on local authorities for failure to spend allocated funding, or removing the responsibility for Traveller accommodation from local authorities and placing it under the authority of a central housing commission.

- More resources should be invested in Traveller education, notably by restoring the visiting teacher service and providing specialised resource teachers. The authorities should raise awareness of the right to free pre-school education among Roma families, and support and encourage participation in early childhood education.
- A national housing strategy should be developed, setting out measures to generate a supply of affordable housing and to combat racial discrimination, with particular attention paid to the needs of all vulnerable communities in the country, including Travellers, Roma, migrants and refugees.
- Sufficient resources should be invested in ensuring that asylum applications are processed more efficiently in order to reduce time spent in Direct Provision; efforts should be made to assist asylum seekers to access the labour market; solutions should be found to LGBT concerns in Direct Provision and the good practices employed in the Mosney Direct Provision centre should be extended to other centres.

In January 2020, the United Nations International Convention on the Elimination of All Forms of Racial Discrimination, CERD, issued its concluding observations on the combined fifth to ninth reports from Ireland. It reiterated a lot of the ECRI report, echoing the following:

Racist hate speech
19. The Committee is concerned about the increasing incidence of racist hate speech directed against Travellers, Roma, refugees, asylum seekers and migrants, in particular through the Internet and social networking platforms. It is also concerned about the frequent incidents of racist hate speech made by politicians, especially during election campaigns. It is further concerned that the Prohibition of Incitement to Hatred Act 1989 has been ineffective in combating racist hate speech, in particular online racist hate speech

Racist hate crime

21. The Committee is concerned about the reportedly high level of racist hate crime targeted at ethnic minorities, which is often in combination with other grounds of discrimination such as gender and religion. While noting the ongoing legislative efforts by the State, the Committee remains concerned that the existing criminal laws of the State do not include substantive racist hate crime offences or provide for aggravating circumstances for such a crime. Consequently, such a crime has not been properly reported and recorded, and the racist motivation of crime has not been systematically taken into consideration throughout criminal proceedings. The Committee is further concerned about the absence of legislation that declares illegal and prohibits racist organisations in the light of the escalation in incidents of far-right rhetoric and racist hate crime targeted at ethnic minority groups.

Nobody can tell me that we Irish are not racist. My rose-tinted glasses have been smashed and I now realise how unconscious, entrenched and insidious racism is in our society. It is so obvious it is almost invisible to many. However our racism is increasingly being identified and challenged. We need to work on that individually and as a country.

At the end of 2020 relevant legislation was passed and subsequently the National Anti-Bullying Research and Resource Centre at Dublin City University was awarded funding by the Department of Justice to establish a new research observatory on cyberbullying. It has a lot to cover. In October 2022 the Criminal Justice (Incitement to Violence or Hatred and Hate Offences) Bill was introduced in the Dáil. It is currently going through the legislative process and hopefully will be signed into law soon.

On 6 February 2023 a prominent anti-refugee protestor in Dublin was charged with offences under Section 2 of the Prohibition of Incitement to Hatred Act 1989. He was charged for distributing material online to stir up hate. While I was delighted to see legislation being used on

113

a far-right aggressor, I was disapointed that it hadn't been used when we were targeted in Lisdoonvarna. Others have been targeted in many communities since. They could have been protected had our abuse been taken seriously and acted upon. The legislation did exist.

Climate and Biodiversity Breakdown

The growing number of climate refugees is a concern. The United Nations reports that since 2008 an average of 21.5 million people have been forcibly displaced annually due to weather-related hazards. It is widely reported that there could be 1.2 billion climate refugees by 2050. The natural world is losing its ability to absorb our pollution. Increasingly, climate and biodiversity breakdown are contributing to migration, directly and indirectly.

I've been working with Irish communities to address climate change since 2007. We brainstorm local solutions to this major challenge. It's how I have come to appreciate the power of collective wisdom, insight and ingenuity. Problem-solving at a community scale allows many more ideas to merge with local knowledge than any national policymaker can even imagine. It is this experience that meant I could play my part in facilitating the community response in Lisdoonvarna.

The greatest obstacle has been government policy, local and national, as well as a lack of cooperation from state agencies and a lack of political will. There are many vested interests making a lot of money who would rather we didn't lower greenhouse gas emissions or protect the environment. They have too much influence and power. They want to continue with business as usual, profit at all costs. We have to be confident enough to not allow these people to get their own way to the detriment of life on Earth, and our children's and grandchildren's wellbeing. We have to stop our government from being persuaded by the economic pressures of these damaging industries and greed. They are driving misery and migration while enjoying a life of abundance.

Every community I have worked with has concluded that we must also build resilience and adapt to the coming changes that we are already locked into based on the global temperature rise to date. In Ireland we are having and will continue to experience stronger storms, more drought and increased rainfall until we find some way to reverse the warming we have contributed to during this fossil-fuelled industrial revolution of the past decades.

Climate action and the transition away from fossil fuels will impact everyone, in all communities. It will be a major test of our ability to collaborate and solve the crisis of our times. Unlike Covid-19, there is no end in sight to the climate and biodiversity emergencies. I have no doubt that a participative, democratic process will give us a much better outcome than the dictatorial, non-participatory approach adopted for Direct Provision.

One example of this was when Ireland's young people sat in the seats of our national elected representatives in Leinster House on 15 November 2019. They collaborated to democratically constitute ten recommendations for the government. They are simple yet effective steps the government can take.

Recommendations to the Dáil by the Youth Assembly on Climate:
» From your corner store to your supermarket, we call on the house to incentivise and obligate the installation of glass doors on open refrigerators.
» For Ireland to ban the importation of fracked gas and invest solely in renewables.
» Implementing measures that will allow Irish goods to be both eco-sustainable and affordable in today's Irish market.
» Implement a tiered tax on emissions from large companies, including those under the capital Emissions Trading Scheme. This tax must be increased every year while the threshold decreases, shifting the burden from individuals to corporations.

» Investment in industrial hemp facilities to provide viable, sustainable and alternative land use for farmers as well as employment in rural Ireland.

» A labelling and pricing system showing the climate impact of food products based on criteria such as impact of packaging and distance travelled.

» Ireland to outlaw acts of ecocide – being the widespread and systematic loss of ecosystems, including climate and cultural damage.

» Protect existing forests and make compulsory that at least 10 per cent of all land owned for agricultural uses is dedicated to forestry.

» A targeted nationwide information campaign to educate the population about the climate crisis regarding causes, effects and solutions.

» Mandatory 'Sustainability' education from primary level to the workplace, including a new compulsory Junior Cycle & optional Leaving Certificate subject.

The numbers of climate refugees will continue to increase. We must make the changes necessary to reduce emissions and lower the global temperature. Our young people are leading the way and we must support them as they seek policy changes in the fight for their future.

For decades, climate scientists, environmental activists and NGOs have been imploring governments to take climate change seriously. We had years of warning to plan a transition away from fossil fuel. Successive governments ignoring those calls means that we now face an abrupt transition instead of a slow and steady process. We must reverse the damage that increased greenhouse gas emissions are doing.

The Direct Provision System

Communities across Ireland have stated that the system of Direct Provision is the reason they protest proposed centres being opened. People in Lisdoonvarna voted to express their opposition to the Direct Provision contract. We, as a community, did nothing to change it except try to stop a centre being opened in our village. The same thing has happened in other communities since.

Are people in the communities who prevented centres from opening doing anything to change the Direct Provision system or are they just sitting back, happy that they stopped a centre being opened in their area? If people are serious about changing the system then there are steps they can take to seek change. Holding the government to account is a good place to start. The 2020 Programme for Government: Our Shared Future states the intention to abolish the Direct Provision system so the political will supposedly exists. Get involved with national and local campaigns to keep up political pressure and ensure that the alternative is not worse.

Covid-19 and Direct Provision

Covid-19 exposed the serious threat that Direct Provision poses to the health of asylum seekers. The centre in Lisdoonvarna took immediate action with strict lockdowns supported by residents. It has meant being confined to one building with 120 or so other people for months. Direct Provision is a major challenge at the best of times but this must have been extremely difficult for many asylum seekers. Especially older children sharing one family room with small siblings. Social media and gaming were a blessing.

Another aspect of Covid-19 and Direct Provision has been the number of asylum seekers who stepped up to work on the front lines during the pandemic. The Minister for Health even thanked them in the Dáil:

> On Direct Provision, first it is really important, for the benefit of those who sometimes like to talk down the many brilliant people who come to our country from other jurisdictions, that we acknowledge that there are 160 healthcare workers resident in Direct Provision centres across the country. When we are applauding and thanking healthcare staff we should be cognisant of the fact that 160 healthcare workers are coming

through Direct Provision. I thank them for the contribution they are making to the Irish health service.

Contrary to that sentiment, in January 2021 two asylum seekers who were working in healthcare during the pandemic received expulsion orders. They were asked to leave the country.

Taken from the MASI website:

The two migrant healthcare workers who initially spoke out against this appalling decision to expel them from Ireland have since been granted leave to remain. The expulsion notices that were served on migrant healthcare workers who had dedicated their lives to protecting vulnerable Irish nationals in nursing homes were simply cruel.

Canada recognised the contribution of migrant workers by offering permanent residency status to healthcare workers. And France is fast-tracking citizenship for migrant healthcare workers. No such schemes have been introduced in Ireland. Instead, we had healthcare workers being told to decide if they are going to leave Ireland voluntarily or be deported.

I have heard many suggestions about how we should provide accommodation. Much like how we need to address our housing and homelessness crisis. We need new homes to be built. We need vacant houses to be bought by the state. The amount of money that is spent on Direct Provision, rent supports and homelessness could provide long-term housing solutions. If social housing were available there would be no need for a big facility contract every time someone was housed. They would just move into the house like everyone else does.

Perhaps instead of putting large numbers of people into rented accommodation in small rural villages we should opt for a small number of state-owned homes in lots of villages and towns? Why don't our local authorities own and manage more homes? Why is money being paid to private enterprises instead of being invested in state-owned housing? Why are taxes going to line the pockets of landlords?

Direct Provision is a profitable business. It cost €183 million in 2020.

If applicants had a decision within three months they wouldn't need Direct Provision for so long. Why is that not happening? Is the current system too lucrative for the accommodation and legal service providers?

Quality of life within a Direct Provision centre depends greatly upon the management. In Lisdoonvarna the organised involvement of the community early on undoubtedly influenced the way asylum seekers have been treated. The community group LINKS has played a major part in being present at the centre and the owner is aware that the wider community cares about what happens inside. Having heard stories from inside other Direct Provision centres around Ireland I believe that we have done good work in Lisdoonvarna, which may make the situation a little less miserable for the residents.

However, no amount of community goodwill could improve life in a hotel room during Covid-19. There were complaints from the general population about having to isolate for two weeks in a hotel as part of a level 5 lockdown during the pandemic. That is nothing compared to spending the whole pandemic in a Direct Provision centre.

There was a consultation in 2019 on the asylum-seeking process and Direct Provision in Ireland. Here are the key recommendations from the submission prepared by MASI, which can be found on their website:

Legal Process: The process of seeking asylum is first and foremost a legal process, so it is essential that people receive all necessary legal advice and that the system is orientated towards vindicating peoples' right to seek asylum and to live in safety.

Work: The right to work must be immediate and unrestricted for all people seeking protection in Ireland.

Reception: People should be accommodated in reception for no longer than three months before moving into housing in the community.

> Direct Provision: Direct provision should be abolished and people seeking asylum in Ireland should have access to the same housing support via their local authorities as is the case for others.
>
> Full and tuition fee-free access to education and training at all levels must be available to international protection applicants.

A working group to report to the government on improvements to the protection process, including Direct Provision, and support to asylum seekers was established, resulting in the McMahon Report in June 2015. On 28 December 2019 the creation of an 'Expert Group on the Provision of Support, including Accommodation, to Persons in the International Protection Process (Asylum Seekers)' was announced. There's also a '2020 Programme for Government Intention to Abolish Direct Provision'. Time will tell what good that will do.

Decision-Making

This is one of my favourite topics. It is inspirational when people come together, information is shared, everyone is heard and decisions are arrived at collaboratively. In my survey in 2019 I asked people in Lisdoonvarna 'How could the Department of Justice and Equality improve the way they operate in relation to communities proposed for a Direct Provision centre?' I have been summarising many of the responses so far but I feel it is worth including everything that the people of Lisdoonvarna suggested the government do to improve how they operate:

- Give me transparent information.
- Advance public notification on a national level; clarity, honesty, a decent debate platform, free legal advice, disclosure of how the location was chosen and why.
- Engage... on all levels... stop steamrolling!

- I actually think providing the people living in Direct Provision with adequate living facilities, i.e. small apartments with cooking facilities, would be better than living in hotel rooms and would drastically improve their quality of life.
- Ensure fitness facilities, i.e. gyms, are easily accessible.
- Also libraries. It's not good for people to live in single rooms.
- Provide mental health services, counselling, upskilling.
- Services would also have to be provided to Irish people who are homeless... that is the majority opinion. Why do we provide for people coming into our country when there are Irish people living on the streets...? Both issues, although different, would have to be seen to be tackled.
- Also, the length of time it takes to process their documentation is a joke... the offices should be expanded and new people hired to help speed up the process, the sooner people get out of Direct Provision the better. It would let them move on with their lives instead of living in a limbo situation.
- Allow no scaremongering.
- Ireland has taken more than its fair share. It's time to start looking after our own people and services.
- Upfront, open and honest.
- Plenty of room for improvements with it.
- End DP would be my first answer, but people should be informed and educated and consulted.
- They could stop the 'dump and run' manner currently used.
- The expectation that communities, mainly rural ones, deal with 'problems', as it were, with little to no funding, experience or knowledge.
- More funding is needed for communities dealing with this inhumane system thrust upon them, although as a community, we've done brilliantly without this.

- It needs to not be treated as a business negotiation, with the owner being paid a ridiculous amount to 'home people'. These are people's lives we're ultimately dealing with.
- I'd love the whole system gone to be honest, and for less harsh or inhumane conditions to come to fruition one day.
- Take no more refugees.
- Engage with the community early & engage in a proper consultation process.
- Meet the locals before the decision is made.
- Stop putting too many people in one place, put smaller numbers in more places, therefore less strain on single doctor practices or crèche places.
- Talk to communities first, to the schools, GPs, local groups – individually and as a whole. Have a Justice and Equality representative liaise with the community before and after. Be accessible.
- Show communities that are against it how successful it has been in other communities. Communication is key, being sly and keeping hush until the asylum seekers are moving in gets people's backs up.
- More support and help for the people that are helping the people in the centre.
- More consultation with local people.
- Information from an official source, detailing what is involved, duration of stay, what type of asylum seeker (family unit, women and children, young adults etc. not race).
- That they don't put these people into hotels. That they provide support for asylum seekers and do not just leave it to the good people in the community to look after them. Proper accommodation should be provided. But they shouldn't receive this before our local people who are on housing waiting lists.
- Make sure appropriate services are available in towns for them.
- Inform much better.
- Consult first, communicate with all the locals and keep everyone in the loop of what's going on.

All of these opinions should have been aired, discussed and mediated before any decision was made. This was a big development within our community that was planned and decided between a government department and a hotel owner. There is absolutely nothing democratic about that.

The initial response was shock, which set the scene for a knee-jerk reaction. The end result could have been an injunction preventing the centre from opening if the inner circle had succeeded. The very basic democratic process that interjected led us onto another path. Other influences could have led to protests, arson or civil unrest, as has happened since. Excluding communities from decisions that affect them is dangerous.

We need participation where people are informed and engage in discussion workshops and brainstorming at localised forums to shape plans for their own community, their county and country. Communities deserve respect and to be listened to. Communication and collaboration are two key aspects to democracy that were effectively non-existent in this process. Elected representatives were totally detached from the decision-making process. We need to reinvent representative democracy.

The fact that we can turn a blind eye to Direct Provision, racism, homelessness, inequality and all the other systemic failures that proliferate in Irish society demonstrates how detached we can be. Can we take intentional, deliberate steps to improve ourselves and our country? Instead of waiting until it becomes an issue that affects us personally or in our own locality.

> I am of the opinion that my life belongs to the whole community and as long as I live, it is my privilege to do for it whatever I can. I want to be thoroughly used up when I die, for the harder I work the more I live.
>
> George Bernard Shaw

7

From Covid-19 to Capitol Hill

The imposition of a centre for Direct Provision kick-started months of unrest in Lisdoonvarna. The government proved that it didn't believe it should consult, or care about what the community had to say. This is common-place in Ireland. I have experienced it firsthand with wind farms and electricity infrastructure in the Midlands, where communities were last to know of plans for their area. All of these situations forced the communities to mobilise and stand up to the government and developers.

The Covid-19 response followed a similar pattern. The situation was very different, as the government was also finding its feet in this global crisis, but there were fundamental similarities. The pandemic came as a shock, there were many questions and the government dictated the response. Denial of the situation was senseless as images of hospitals under enormous pressure in China and Italy were all over most media. Various levels of restrictions and lockdowns were introduced in the hope that they would prevent people spreading the highly infectious virus to vulnerable people. One major concern was the prospect of Ireland's under-resourced healthcare system being overloaded.

When the government imposed restrictions most people accepted them, but they were also questioned and rejected by some. Some people were convinced that the statistics, media coverage, human stories, documentaries and so on were rigged or invented. Theories ranged from Covid-19 being a conspiracy about the 'New World Order' plotting the 'Great Reset', to being a plan for world domination by technology companies who would insert microchips into people through vaccines. Many of these suggestions came from the far right. While not everyone who questioned the Covid-19 response was far-right, the far right stepped up as opposition to the measures and actively set about recruiting.

One common denominator for the far right with Covid-19 was a focus on 'freedom'. They championed the narrative that our freedom was being denied and organised or hijacked protests against restrictions. This introduced new followers and supporters to a movement that had been spreading lies, hatred and racism for the previous two years. People oblivious to this movement's earlier campaigns and core principles were recruited as they rallied against lockdown, masks and social distancing.

One very contentious and emotive issue was vaccines. With companies scrambling to get the vaccines made and countries eagerly awaiting them, fears about mandatory vaccination grew. While those concerned about vaccines, free speech and restrictions attended 'freedom' protests, they were also giving an audience to far-right leaders and mobilisers, signing up to their campaigns and social media outlets.

The pandemic further demonstrated the online echo chamber effect. As people sought answers and followed leads, many 'experts' with a variety of explanations enticed them to spend their time in lockdown reading, following or listening to them. For months social media facilitated the mass sharing of misinformation while their software and algorithms continued to supply those seeking oppositional 'evidence'.

While I shared information about how to get support during the pandemic, I also received messages about how I was a 'covidiot' or one of the 'sheeple' of the 'plandemic'. I had Covid conspiracy debates with a number of friends, including the friend I had accompanied to my first town hall meeting about Direct Provision. The division became very real as I watched friends sharing articles from the same far-right sources that had attacked our community. People closely involved with welcoming asylum seekers to Lisdoonvarna have followed the path of disinformation. Two of them are actively protesting about and spreading conspiracies. They went from being targeted by the far right to amplifying their lies.

Far-right groups and political parties that had focused on Lisdoon-varna were now denying the pandemic, but it was even more worrying that they were attracting people they had targeted for caring about asylum seekers. The same people who came to Lisdoonvarna to stoke hatred and fear went on to mobilise and support other protesters, bringing with them their core anti-democratic, divisive, regressive, homophobic beliefs and violence. The same people were organising 'freedom' protests during the Covid-19 pandemic.

When media and social media standards were introduced to check facts relating to Covid-19, the far right claimed free speech was being silenced. All Covid articles and posts were given a virtual warning label until the source was checked and the information verified. This was a measure to curtail the increasing spread of misinformation. This fact-checking cost social media companies millions but introduced new measures in corporate social responsibility.

Should we question science? Should we question the media? Should we question medicine? Should we question the government? Yes, of course we should and trusted sources are the necessary foundation when looking for answers. Should we question ourselves? Definitely!

It is easy to see how the far-right message can be attractive. They oppose the generic issues practically everyone opposes, such as crime, corruption, anti-social behaviour and paedophilia. There is often a grain of truth in what they say. Covid-19 restrictions, for example, obviously impact freedom, and vaccine programmes are commonplace. However, we live in a democracy where we have a choice about vaccines. During

Covid-19 many people with very valid concerns and well-meaning intentions followed a beacon they might not have normally followed.

Eager to garner as much support as possible, the far right preyed on people's concerns during the pandemic and organised the 'freedom' protests and marches. As they protested they taunted and intimidated people who were wearing masks. During at least two of the events in Dublin, violence broke out and protesters used concealed weapons and combat gear that they were wearing, such as studded gloves and hammers. I have been at many protests and counter-protests in Ireland over several decades and I have never encountered violence. Ever.

The following is a small excerpt from an *Irish Times* article dated 19 September 2020 titled:

The far right rises: Its growth as a political force in Ireland
By Conor Gallagher

IT REMAINS A FRAGMENTED MINORITY MOVEMENT IN IRELAND, BUT THE FAR RIGHT IS EXPLOITING THE COVID-19 CRISIS TO EXTEND ITS INFLUENCE – ONLINE AND ON THE STREET

Shortly after 3 p.m. last Saturday, messaging accounts belonging to Ireland's most active far-right activists began to light up with glee.

'Ever see a lesbian bleed before?' a poster named 'Irelands Woes' asked their 1,650 subscribers. 'The left must have a fetish for getting beaten up,' said another poster calling themselves 'Edgy memes na hÉireann'.

Their joy on Saturday was caused by an assault on a veteran LGBT+ campaigner, K, who had been attacked while counter-protesting an anti-face mask rally outside Leinster House. K was hit by a piece of wood wrapped in a tricolour, leaving her with a nasty head wound that required hospital treatment.

The words of the posters are almost as ugly as the attack itself. The people who wrote them are part of what experts and gardaí believe is a growing far-right movement in Ireland – one that is attempting to hijack social concerns in a bid for the mainstream support.

The last five words sum it up nicely: 'a bid for mainstream support'. That is effectively what I have witnessed the far right doing ever since they imposed themselves upon Lisdoonvarna in 2018.

There was violence at protests twice that month. A return to violent protest is not a good indicator for our democracy. The far right organised under the banner of 'freedom' while aggressively silencing anyone they didn't want to hear. They have been spreading lies, hatred and racism in Ireland. They target anyone with opposing values or opinions. That is fascism.

The Merrian-Webster Dictionary defines fascism as:

a political philosophy, movement, or regime (such as that of the Fascisti) that exalts nation and often race above the individual and that stands for a centralized autocratic government headed by a dictatorial leader, severe economic and social regimentation, and forcible suppression of opposition.

Corruption, incompetence and injustice have been eroding trust in the Irish government for decades. Every new scandal that hits the media, every mention of the bank bailout, cervical checks, institutional abuse, FAS, money 'resting' in politicians' bank accounts, whistle-blower abuse, quangos, industry-led policy, Ireland being a corporate tax haven, clerical sex abuse, the latest homeless crisis, suicide and hospital trolley statistics, all provide many reasons to not trust the government. They all provide many reasons to be angry with the government. The disillusionment, anger and lack of trust all present openings for the far right.

The violence and death that occurred at the United States Capitol on 6 January 2021 was fuelled by far-right messaging on social media. Members of Congress feared for their lives as they rushed to find safety when thousands of lawless Trump supporters, conspiracy theorists, white supremacists and more broke into the building. They were seeking 'justice' for Trump's fictitious claims of a stolen election and calls for retaliation. It was a blatant rejection of and attack on democracy, building on four years of racist, homophobic, misogynistic messaging. It was fascism. The city was in chaos, elected officials and staff were terrorised and at least five people died because of this mobilisation to #stopthesteal. The world watched while the symbolic heart of American democracy was attacked.

A week later the same house voted to impeach the outgoing president, Donald Trump, for his role in that violence with a charge of incitement of insurrection.

Throughout his four-year term, Trump used social media to spread lies, racism, misogyny, division, fascism and incitement to violence. He abused his position to pursue his fascist agenda. On 6 January 2020 both Twitter and Facebook suspended his accounts. I wonder why it took so long.

On 7 January, a statement from Facebook declared:

> The shocking events of the last 24 hours clearly demonstrate that President Donald Trump intends to use his remaining time in office to undermine the peaceful and lawful transition of power to his elected successor, Joe Biden. We believe the risks of allowing the President to continue to use our service during this period are simply too great. Therefore, we are extending the block we have placed on his Facebook and Instagram accounts indefinitely and for at least the next two weeks until the peaceful transition of power is complete.

This was Facebook confirming that their platform can play a part in disrupting peace and law.

Twitter permanently suspended Trump's account due to the risk of further incitement of violence. They judged that his tweets on 8 January had breached their Glorification of Violence policy.

The following analysis is taken from Twitter and explains how his words could be interpreted as inciting violence.

Trump's tweet on 8 January read:

> The 75,000,000 great American Patriots who voted for me, AMERICA FIRST, and MAKE AMERICA GREAT AGAIN, will have a GIANT VOICE long into the future. They will not be disrespected or treated unfairly in any way, shape or form!!!

Shortly thereafter, he tweeted:

> To all of those who have asked, I will not be going to the Inauguration on January 20th.

This was Twitter's analysis of his tweets and the reasoning behind the ban:

> This determination is based on a number of factors, including:
>   President Trump's statement that he will not be attending the Inauguration is being received by a number of his supporters as further confirmation that the election was not legitimate and is seen as him disavowing his previous claim made via two Tweets (1, 2) by his Deputy Chief of Staff, Dan Scavino, that there would be an 'orderly transition' on January 20th.
>   The second Tweet may also serve as encouragement to those potentially considering violent acts that the Inauguration would be a 'safe' target, as he will not be attending.
>   The use of the words 'American Patriots' to describe some of his supporters is also being interpreted as support for those committing violent acts at the US Capitol.

The mention of his supporters having a 'GIANT VOICE long into the future' and that 'They will not be disrespected or treated unfairly in any way, shape or form!!!' is being interpreted as further indication that President Trump does not plan to facilitate an 'orderly transition' and instead that he plans to continue to support, empower, and shield those who believe he won the election.

Plans for future armed protests have already begun proliferating on and off-Twitter, including a proposed secondary attack on the US Capitol and state capitol buildings on January 17, 2021.

As such, our determination is that the two Tweets above are likely to inspire others to replicate the violent acts that took place on January 6, 2021, and that there are multiple indicators that they are being received and understood as encouragement to do so.

In February 2016 Twitter deleted 125,000 Isis accounts as an anti-terrorism measure. In January 2020 it deleted 70,000 accounts following the attack on Capitol Hill.

This was Twitter confirming that their platform can play a part in glorifying violence and terrorism.

Both Facebook and Twitter brought in emergency measures to prevent their platforms being used to spread misinformation or incite further violence ahead of Joe Biden's inauguration. Facebook continued with measures introduced ahead of the election and introduced more, including automatically disabling comments in groups with high rates of hate speech or content that incites violence; using artificial intelligence to demote content that violates policies and increasing the requirement of group admins to review and approve posts before they go up. Within days, further measures were introduced, from blocking the creation of new events in the US Capitol to banning ads promoting weapon accessories and protective equipment.

This is all well and good after the fact but how many people had already formed allegiances using these platforms? These allies have simply moved on to different platforms to continue their hatred with a new sense of victimisation and thirst for retaliation.

The ease with which American democracy descended into chaos is worrying. It demonstrated the trajectory this echo chamber division follows, confirmed our concerns in Lisdoonvarna and validated my decision to write this book. The messaging and much of the organising was done in plain sight. This is also happening in Ireland. I cannot overstate the role of social media in magnifying messages, good and bad. When the so-called 'leader of the free world' can continue in power, having acquired a reputation for inciting hatred and violence while in office, then go on to incite a violent insurrection when he loses power, something is fundamentally wrong.

Two years and two days later, on 8 January 2023, supporters of the defeated Brazilian far-right president, Jair Bolsonaro, executed their own insurrection, invading the Congress, presidential palace and Supreme Court in Brasilia, and calling for the military to reinstate Bolsonaro as president and imprison the newly elected Lula da Silva. Fascism is infectious.

The Irish general election of 2020 was testament to the fact that people of Ireland wanted change. Surely if a lot of right-wing policies are reactionary and seek to prevent certain changes, then true change means moving away from the dominance of right-wing politics, not deeper into it. Voters did that as they increased their votes for left-wing parties in 2020.

Should we still categorise our politics in line with the French Revolution? Could we evolve from a right or left position? Can we find better ways to collaborate? A lot has changed in two hundred years. We need to explore new ways of operating within participatory processes. We need systems designed for the twenty-first century.

In October 2022 Twitter was bought by Elon Musk, who went on to fire almost half of the workforce, including the team who were there to monitor hate speech. He reversed the ban placed on Trump and reinstated other well-known far-right actors, including many in Ireland, some of whom I have referred to earlier in this book. Within hours of his takeover, use of the N-word increased by almost 500 per cent. Transphobic, misogynistic and anti-semitic language also surged.

We must hold social media and software companies to account. However, it needs to be the government that sets the agenda because Twitter has shown that self-regulation only works when the management cares. Social media is facilitating the spread of misinformation and fuelling polarisation. It enables the glorification of violence and terrorism. It incites violence. Companies have said so themselves.

> May I stress the need for courageous, intelligent and dedicated leadership... Leaders of sound integrity. Leaders not in love with publicity, but in love with justice. Leaders not in love with money, but in love with humanity.
>
> Dr Martin Luther King, Jr.

8

Wrapping Up

Residents of the Direct Provision centre had seen the media coverage of the opposition to their arrival while they were preparing and travelling to Lisdoonvarna. They were worried about coming to our village and feared for their safety. A warm welcome from the community eased their concerns and helped to change their opinion.

When the wider community was asked 'How do you feel about the Direct Provision centre in Lisdoonvarna 19 months later?' most people who responded had accepted the centre in the village. They were positive about the residents, while detesting the system of Direct Provision and the process through which the centre was established. People expressed empathy for the residents having to live there. A good few people were concerned about the impact on the children, including the length of time they live in Direct Provision and their ability to support friendships outside of school.

I am very proud of the people of Lisdoonvarna and beyond. Their initial shock reaction did not control their final response. They proved that at the very core of Irish people is a deep sense of community and that we can come together with compassion. Although we were caught unawares by the plan to locate the centre in our village, we knew who was not at fault and were ready to help those who needed us. We also challenged the incompetence of those who deserved to be challenged. We rejected the hateful messaging and lies of the far right. We were targeted by fascists and held our ground. People came together to make life for our new neighbours a little better than it might otherwise have been.

Community

Plenty has happened since March 2018. A mother and toddler group was established at the centre and opened to the wider community. There's a vegetable garden on site that welcomes the wider community. Residents also volunteer locally with clean-ups in the park or don the yellow vest to join the Tidy Towns group. Many of the children participate in the local sports clubs, including summer camps.

Many of the women have been involved with the Clare Women's Collective and have had opportunities to politicise their lived experiences as feminist issues. By speaking at events on important feminist issues, such as violence against women, racism, exclusion and being 'othered', they also have opportunities to educate white and indigenous Irish people on cultures outside of their own experiences, which has deeply enriched the lives of the listeners. This has enhanced possibilities for engagement, progression and for natural integration to begin to take root in an authentic way in rural Ireland. Some of the women have gone on to participate in developing significant projects in Clare related to exploring white privilege and increasing the visibility of the LGBT+ community, for example.

Clare Local Development Company continues to do great work under the Social Inclusion Community Activation Programme. The homework club they organise at the school two days a week is supplemented by the centre providing homework support on the other two days. Clare PPN has hosted various information events for residents. They also facilitated participation in the local elections, with an evening to meet the candidates and register to vote. Many asylum seekers participate in education, ranging from English language lessons to university courses.

There have been some capital projects in the village. The local community crèche has an extension, the primary school has a new AstroTurf pitch and the community centre has a new kitchen. When work permits came through, there was a form of employment fair at the centre. A lot of residents have found employment with local businesses in North Clare during the tourist season.

When Covid-19 impacted our lives, bringing many activities to a halt, the community of Lisdoonvarna and North Clare responded very quickly. They excelled with ideas and actions that helped with wellbeing and caring. Our experience with Direct Provision, the communication channels it opened up and the collaboration it generated have served us well.

In January 2023, almost five years after the news broke of the Direct Provision plans, over 900 Ukrainians are living in Lisdoonvarna. The invasion of Ukraine by Russia resulted in mass displacement and there is no doubt that what happened in 2018 somewhat prepared Lisdoonvarna for this challenge. Five more establishments are accommodating refugees. Along with keeping the accommodation providers in business, there has been a lot of employment locally as numbers attending school and needing services expand. A new bus route with an additional four runs is in operation. The park has been upgraded and there are four new pedestrian crossings. Land has been identified for a new, long overdue, secondary school. Perhaps these improvements are coincidental but I'm pretty sure some of them, if not all, were helped along by our capacity for caring as a community.

Nationally we have major challenges with rural isolation and loneliness. For some local people in Lisdoonvarna, our coffee mornings are the only social activity they attend.

People often fall through the cracks, but it is possible to fill those cracks. Caring communities nurture spaces so people know they always have somewhere to go. Not everybody plays a sport or goes to church, so it's important to make other social options available. We can build our communities to be inclusive.

Recommendation

Build community? Start with solid foundations, such as a baby and toddler group. Have affordable places for children to meet up, such as homework clubs and music, drama and summer camps, dedicated play and hang-out areas, activity-based groups and youth clubs. Have somewhere for parents to meet. Put in seating that encourages communication somewhere accessible. Every community could have a writers' group, community garden, walking club, women's groups, bingo, dancing, a community cafe, a men's shed, as well as an active retirement group and more. Caring for our community is helped when we have places to meet, especially with tea! Take the time to invest in the social infrastructure that works for your community, even if it's not directly relevant to you. All the facilities in the world don't matter if the social fibre is frayed. Build relationships. Nurture caring. It takes a village to raise a child and a community to see them through life.

How a community treats its most vulnerable is an excellent measure of how caring it is, and we can do a lot to nurture an inclusive, caring, resilient community.

Consultation

One lesson from Direct Provision is that the government's drop-and-run practice must be challenged. They might promise the schools, crèche and doctor additional resources, but what about the ordinary people within the community? The people who are on the frontlines, doing what they can to help steady the ship, who are targeted by extremists, helping integration when the asylum seekers are not in school, crèche or sick? In Lisdoonvarna we were let down from the start.

What happened in Lisdoonvarna went on to happen across the country. The government's approach was absolutely flawed and their failings placed people in the firing line of the far right. This format was totally disempowering and fuelled anger. The community felt excluded, irrelevant and betrayed.

This problem is not limited to Direct Provision. Communities are disempowered by decisions being made for them on a regular basis. There is a democratic deficit nationally.

Recommendation:

Non-consultation and tick box consultation processes must be replaced by comprehensive public participation, including facilitated discussion, problem-solving and brainstorming at the community level to inform local, regional and national plans. Information on plans that affect a community must be forthcoming, transparent and delivered in their entirety.

Participation

There are still intersectional issues that need to be addressed. We need social outcry to challenge each issue; public participation to help solve the issues and the political will to support and drive the changes deemed necessary. We must have people-centred solutions instead of market-centred profits. We need whole systems, joined up thinking with interdepartmental, society-wide collaboration.

We need the silent majority to engage in a participative, democratic process. I say that as someone who has engaged in activism for decades, helping to shape Irish policy and facilitating sustainable community development. We really need everyone at the table shaping the Ireland we want.

A lot more needs to be done to engage people at the community level and bring them into the critical thinking and decision-making process. In theory, at the moment engagement in policy at the local and national level affords everyone the opportunity to shape it. This can be done through Public Participation Networks, NGOs, individual engagement or other bodies representing society at decision-making tables around the country. However, that is too far removed from many people and communities, especially in rural Ireland.

Instead of having decisions imposed on them, people should be afforded the respect, trust and opportunity to proactively engage in the changes we need to make, whether that be in response to a local issue or part of a national vision. Everybody needs to have their say. Solutions will come from the people and a top-down, bottom-up approach has a greater probability of delivering much more successful outcomes.

Recommendation:

Establish systems for local, participative democracy. Given the challenges we face, especially the climate and biodiversity crises, I believe that an inclusive, collaborative, sustainable development forum is essential in every community.

Communication

The far right have proven themselves insidious as they repeatedly infiltrate, fuel the fear, align with the doubters and manipulate the community response. The hands-off approach by the government allows the far right to swoop in and feed on the community's disorientation. It allows lies to spread that confuse and mislead people at a time when people are vulnerable. What could the government have done to support and protect volunteers who were trying to act on the facts while debunking the lies and misinformation?

Similar tactics were used by the far right during the referendum to Repeal the Eighth Amendment and during the Covid-19 crisis. Lies, half-truths and misinformation were allowed to spread online unless software companies or media outlets challenged them.

We live in a time when information can be shared with anyone anywhere in the world within seconds. While that has amazing benefits it is also dangerous. A person can go down a rabbit hole of untruths as easily as find the facts. Without credible validation of the facts and exposure of the lies by a trusted source, anyone can abuse the information superhighway.

Due to the critical threat posed by Covid-19, the government communicated facts regularly across many platforms. It was very effective at encouraging people to take precautions and mobilised volunteers to help their community. Having experienced climate denial for decades and been unsupported by the government, I wonder when they will treat the climate and biodiversity crises with the same vigour as they have shown during Covid-19.

Recommendation:

Whether it relates to matters of national or local importance the government needs to provide adequate, accurate information across many platforms to ensure that the facts are readily available. They must take steps to stop the spread of misinformation and lies. This includes compelling social media companies to play their part.

Infiltration

The government must take the threat the far right pose to our peaceful society seriously. For years people have been sounding the alarm that their messages of hatred and intolerance needed to be met with strong state opposition. Many people, including me, have been threatened by aggressors for highlighting their behaviour. We do this in order to prevent people being sucked in by them. In the absence of state oversight and response it has been left to individuals and the media to highlight their agitating and aggression. The situation is escalating and they are becoming increasingly confident. Acts of intimidation are increasing and they regularly incite violence, arson and the use of weapons.

Recommendation:

There is hate legislation in Ireland. Improve it and use it.

Finally

I have absolutely no hesitation in saying that the way the Direct Provision centre was imposed in Lisdoonvarna caused massive trauma in my community and to me personally. It was extremely divisive. People didn't know what to believe in the absence of official information and with decisions made behind a veil of secrecy. None of the official leaders – elected representatives or council staff – came into play. Nobody known and trusted by the community was available to them when this news broke. It left the gates wide open for manipulators to deliver their message of intolerance.

It felt strangely familiar when the Ukrainian refugees arrived just before St Patrick's Day 2022. I remembered that the hotelier had said to me in 2018 that St Patrick's Day was the first time he had seen some of the asylum seekers smiling. Life was very busy for me at the time because my mother was very sick but I felt I would be able to arrange some face painting. So, as we had done in 2018, we arrived at the hotels with face paints, creating distraction and hopefully bringing a smile to some faces, if only for a moment. It was a beautiful day as the sun shone down on our celebrations. In 2022 the asylum seekers had their own floats and the Ukrainian refugees lined the streets at their first community event. I really hoped that the small offering of face paints and attempt at inclusion helped to lighten the mood for a little while.

I participated in the parade with the Lisdoonvarna Tidy Towns team, who handed out sunflower seeds while marching through the village. The sunflower is the national flower of Ukraine. Having spent too long painting faces, I was late to the parade and found myself at the very back carrying the Irish tricolour and Ukrainian flags that I had put on bamboo canes. When I turned at the top of the town to follow the parade back down the main street a woman from Ukraine, Katryn, came over and asked if she could carry the Ukrainian flag. That was a really magical moment for me. It's very hard to explain how much it meant. I was so happy that she felt safe enough to approach me to ask and I felt very proud that I had the flag in the first place. As we walked and talked, I noticed the smiling faces on the children lining the street. I was listening to Katryn's traumatic experience while aware that our parade had helped some children to smile for a little while. A photo of us walking side by side with our respective flags was printed in the *Clare Champion* the following week.

It's not all rainbows and roses. In 2022 Clare PPN published a great report on poverty in the county which paints a clearer picture of life for many people. We lack affordable homes, healthcare, dental care and more. These issues are not new but they do need to be addressed urgently for the sake of everyone living in Lisdoonvarna.

The importance of the silent majority cannot be overstated. I ask that people have the confidence to become informed, stand up and be counted. I want people to dare to care about all of these issues and engage with the changes we need to make. Engage with those leading the call for change from a human rights perspective and not the far right. Stand up. Speak up.

I notice that local people are getting more vocal in their opposition to the hatred. The far-right agitators are being identified. Some people are more trusting of the far right, having followed them during the pandemic. Hopefully they will see the hate and mobilise independently or support existing bodies calling for change. The violence and aggression haven't stopped though, as some people are still following them blindly in the void created by the lack of information and reassurance from the government. They are still stirring up hatred, most recently in a number of places in Dublin and Shannon in Clare.

The far right seek to exploit people's concerns and any possible platform to spread their messages. They speak about freedom, Ireland as a united nation, patriotism, the Irish people, equality, democracy and use all of the romantic language we heard in history class. They exploit the genuine need for change around issues that people are passionate about, such as housing, homelessness, healthcare and poverty. Their solution is to scapegoat asylum seekers and refugees rather than blame failed government policies. Their tactics have brought fear, aggression and violence to Ireland.

A closer look at them reveals a vision that would return us to the Ireland of our history books. Their vision goes against issues that the people of Ireland have voted on, such as divorce, same-sex marriage and abortion.

They speak about freedom but they could not tolerate my free speech or that of others. They oppose evictions, but only if it is Irish people being evicted. They preach democracy, yet twisted the democratic response in Lisdoonvarna to suit their racist agenda. They mention equality but their policies support some lives being worth less than others. They allude to Ireland belonging to the Irish yet ignore the wishes of the Irish people.

To my fellow change-makers and activists: I ask that you be careful who you align with. Seeking justice is hard work and change is long overdue but we must ensure that those who drive change have a social conscience. I hope that homelessness, racism, ecocide, climate break-down, Direct Provision, healthcare, corruption and the circumstances facilitating the rise of the far right in Ireland are tackled immediately with solutions that respect everybody equally.

While I used the word 'crossroads' in the title of this book, in reality it is an intersection. All of these big issues overlap and there is a core theme. People have been exploited, murdered and persecuted to enable a small percentage of the global population to amass wealth while destroying our shared planet. In all of these issues someone is getting rich.

There is a shift. A growing movement of caring, of people of every gender, young and old, seeking change for the greater good. Recognising that collaboration is our greatest strength and route to the power that matters, the power to sort this mess out. But the greed, wealth and domination must stop.

We must rock the systems that need to be changed. We must nurture care, compassion and unity while creating a future worthy of our children and their children. We must have active citizens in every community to make sure the changes needed actually happen.

Theresa x

> Alone we can do so little; together we can do so much.
> Helen Keller

Postscript

As we go to press in March 2023 this same pattern is playing out in Shannon, another town in Clare. Rumours broke that a warehouse was to be used to house refugees. The conversations were predictable, with all sorts of guesses being made about the numbers, origin and sex of the asylum seekers. Fears are being fuelled with words and phrases like 'military-aged men', 'unvetted', 'rape' and 'violence' being bandied about. The saying 'I'm not racist but ...' is heard regularly. On 4 March 2023 there was a silent protest and up to 30 people of the 10,000 residents in Shannon attended. Their yellow signs resembled those of the group who protest at a roundabout in Ennis most weekends.

In Lisdoonvarna we have had some infrastructural improvements, but we still have no additional doctors or a dentist. We have more people seeking homes with no additional houses. The government is failing to provide the essential services and people are becoming less tolerant of the situation. We also have a growing far-right presence locally. There is suspicion about plans to develop social housing, claiming it is a plot to build modular homes for refugees. There are claims of a prostitution ring and that anti-social behaviour is rampant – all being spread by people who believe that Covid-19 was a plan to murder the population, that Russia didn't invade Ukraine and that climate change is a power grab by the World Economic Forum.

Postscript

In North Clare we have the chairman of the Irish Freedom Party, a founder of Breitbart media and the chairman of the Irish Republican Brotherhood, who recently wrote to the British Prime Minister to tell him that their president is in fact the president of the sovereign state of Éire. The IRB believe that they are the true agents of the state and have a whole webpage linking far-right propaganda channels and conspiracy theorists.

We have a well-organised anti-racism network in Clare who are very well informed about the far right. Four women, suspected of being involved with the network, recently had their photos and details shared within far-right circles. The 'Asylum Industry' video is still in circulation pointing towards Clare PPN and myself as government agents.

Nationally a new far-right political party, Ireland First, has emerged. Having looked at their website, it appears to consist of one person, a well-known agitator. Far-right men are menacingly patrolling the streets saying they are protecting women. Yet they have proven many times that they target women who reject them. Violence has returned to our streets as fascism rises.

On 18 February 2023, up to 50,000 people marched against racism in Dublin using the slogan #IrelandForAll. A colourful group travelled from Clare with our megaphone, flags and custom chant 'from the Shannon to the sea, keep the Banner fascist free'. County Clare is often nicknamed 'the Banner county'. The following week a far-right protest, #IrelandIsFull, couldn't get one thousand people. These are positive signs that fascism is being rejected by the majority of Irish people.

The government is failing to provide housing, healthcare and more. They cannot be trusted to deliver society's needs. Recently the Taoiseach referred to the far right and extreme left as though they were equally abhorrent. Playing politics. The reality is that the government has failed to protect us from the far right and is acting in a way that increases their popularity. The task of countering fascism has had to be taken on by the left, who patrol social media, raise awareness by unmasking the hatred, and organise counter-protests.

Acknowledgements

Many thanks to Eamon Ward for the image of the flier attached to the front door of the hotel.

Thank you to Clare FM who were happy for me to reproduce the content from their website. Also for the way they handled the situation in Lisdoonvarna. It was very professional and balanced.

http://www.clare.fm/news/lisdoonvarna-hotel-accommodate-asylum-seekers/

Thank you to the Clare Champion for permission to use their article and their coverage of our stories.

https://clarechampion.ie/heated-views-at-lisdoonvarna-Direct-Provision-public-meeting/

Thank you to Gordon Deegan, Sorcha Pollak and Conor Gallagher for permission to include their insightful articles. Thank you to the *Irish Times* for agreeing.

https://www.irishtimes.com/news/social-affairs/we-are-against-Direct-Provision-and-how-it-was-forced-on-us-1.3421404

https://www.irishtimes.com/news/ireland/irish-news/how-the-far-right-is-exploiting-immigration-concerns-in-oughterard-1.4026612

https://www.irishtimes.com/news/ireland/irish-news/the-far-right-rises-its-growth-as-a-political-force-in-ireland-1.4358321

Many thanks to Rubber Bandits for the use of their tweet.

Acknowledgements

Thank you to everyone who contributed towards the costs of producing this book. I hope it will help others when their community is in the limelight and help people recognise far-right agitators. Thanks to Martin for all your support and help.

Thank you to Erin Darcy whose book *In Her Shoes – Women of the Eighth* was published in autumn 2020, with New Island Books. It is her story of community, activism, motherhood, grief, trauma, belonging and her art project that became a pivotal part of the campaign to Repeal the Eighth Amendment. You can order it at www.newisland.ie.

Thank you to the people of Lisdoonvarna. You have proved that community matters. We did well and care won out in the end.

I wish to thank and acknowledge the Movement of Asylum Seekers in Ireland for all the work they do.

MASI - the Movement of Asylum Seekers in Ireland. Comments on the government's response to Covid-19 in Direct Provision can be found at the following URL.

https://www.masi.ie/wp-content/uploads/2020/06/RESPONSE-TO-COVID-19-IN-DIRECT-PROVISION-FINAL.pdf

Thank you to Clare PPN (Public Participation Network) for all the support, guidance and practical help shown over the years.

Thank you to my many proofreaders – see, I was listening! You really, really helped.

Appendix 1

Community questions were gathered on Monday 26 February and the answers were received on Wednesday 28 February.

Q: Is the contract signed?
A: The Minister for Justice and Equality has concluded a contract with the proprietors of the hotel.

Q: Who decided that Lisdoonvarna would be a host village?
A: On 8 January 2018 RIA published a notice in the national papers and the *EU Journal* seeking expressions of interest from businesses who were in a position to offer full board accommodation on behalf of the State to persons seeking international protection. As a result of that call for expressions of interest, the hotel was offered to the department.

Q: Does the hotel owner still own the hotel or has it been sold recently?
A: We are not aware of any change in the ownership of the hotel.

Q: Who is expected to sign a contract to feed and care for the asylum seekers?
A:The contract covers full board and accommodation for all residents in the accommodation centre in a hotel type environment.

Appendix 1

Q: Is there a per capita cut off on numbers housed? We would have the highest ratio of locals to asylum seekers in the country. What about the population increase and support for new parents amongst the asylum seekers?

A: No. There is no per capita limit. However in the case of Lisdoonvarna it must be noted that there are at least four hotels operational for a good part of the year. Bearing in mind the responses given to other questions, the addition of a maximum of 115 persons over the course of a year should not put an undue strain on existing resources and services.

Q: Why were we not consulted before last week? Why the secrecy?

A: The notices were published in the press on 8 January 2018 with a closing date of 26 January 2018. The contractual discussions concluded on Friday 16 February. Public representatives were notified on Tuesday 20 February. There is no secrecy.

Q: Can the implementation be put back a few months?

A: No. The only reason we have put back the opening by a week is because of the current weather situation, which in turn prevents us from attending the meeting on Wednesday 28 February. We still have an increasing demand for accommodation.

Q: Is the second group of 30 being deferred as promised?

A: Our intention is to accommodate 30 persons per month until we have reached capacity at the accommodation centre.

Q: Can the allocation be capped at 30?

A: The contract is for a maximum of 115 persons.

Q: Is planning secured for change of use?

A: This is an exempt development for planning purposes.

Q: Has the fire officer inspected the premises to ensure all fire regulations in relation to change of use are met?

A: The local authority has confirmed that there are no issues in relation to the fire certification on this premises.

Q: Will the asylum seekers be housed in Lisdoonvarna without support?
A: No. Supports from government offices and agencies, NGOs, volunteers and the local community will be provided (as is the case right across all 34 accommodation centres around the country).

Q: Will they be provided with healthy, balanced meals? Do they have a say in what their meals are?
A: It is a contractual requirement that meals are nutritional and that the ethnic and cultural needs of the residents are met. The menu runs on a 28-day cycle and includes vegetarian options at all meals. Tea/coffee and snacks are available on a 24/7 basis.

Q: Will their participation in community activities be funded – equipment, gear etc.?
A: This will be examined on a case-by-case basis.

Q: Will they receive counselling for psychological issues arising from their experiences?
A: Please see the separate note below from the HSE about all medical services.

Q: Could there be opposing groups housed in the centre? Enemies?
A: No. RIA ensures that the allocation of persons to accommodation centres takes account of ethnic, religious and cultural issues. Having said that, it is a requirement for all residents to treat all other persons with dignity and respect.

Q: What provision is there for language training to enable integration?
A: English language training is provided on-site to adults by the local ETB. English language supports are provided to school children through the

established EAL (English as an Additional Language) support services in schools.

Q: Can the residents cook for themselves?
A: All food is prepared and served by qualified hotel staff. Residents will be consulted about their meals to ensure that they are ethnically and culturally appropriate.

Q: Can they look after the garden at the hotel or in the community?
A: If they wish to do so, why not!

Q: Do the residents have basic family time, such as sitting down to a meal together?
A: Yes – mealtimes are set to suit the residents within reason.

Q: Can the residents volunteer in the community? During September perhaps?
A: If they wish to do so – why not! Residents are free to come and go from their accommodation as they wish. They are also free to engage and participate in any aspect of community life as they wish.

Q: What will be done to stop them suffering from being stuck in a hotel?
A: In all of our accommodation centres we have established a group called 'Friends of the Centre'. These groups comprise local NGOs and volunteers (everything from football clubs to homework clubs to poetry to painting and hand crafts) and work with residents to establish friendships and activities.

Q: Can the children join local clubs? Community games?
A: Yes. Subject to parental control (and all children are with their parents) children are free to come and go from their accommodation as they wish. They are also free to engage and participate in any aspect of community life as they wish.

Appendix 1

Q: Can the residents work?

A: Persons who are in the protection process for more than nine months and who have cooperated with the process will be given an entitlement to access the labour market. This will be introduced in June of 2018.

Q: How do residents integrate elsewhere?

A: By joining local clubs, gyms, societies, sports etc. residents are not detained in any way in the accommodation centre. They are free to come and go from their accommodation as they wish. They are also free to engage and participate in any aspect of community life as they wish.

Q: Are there any asylum seekers who have been refused admission elsewhere? In the UK?

A: No – all these persons have applied for international protection in Ireland.

Q: What nationality are they?

A: Applicants come from all over the world – Bangladesh, Venezuela, the Democratic Republic of the Congo, Georgia, Zimbabwe, Kuwait, Mauritius, etc. In Ireland, there is a legal prohibition on identifying any person as being an applicant for international protection.

Q: Are they all families? How many are in family units?

A: Only families (or single females) will be accommodated in the accommodation centres in Lisdoonvarna. Family units will be quite small.

Q: What is the age breakdown? There are concerns about the concentration of one age group, especially young males and orphans. Will our schools be supported, given the resources and facilities they need? Will they have help with language at school and other services?

A: As in all other accommodation centres, the Department of Education and Tusla will work with local schools to ensure that all supports are provided. Specifically in relation to the first group due to arrive on 12

Appendix 1

March 2018 there are seven children in total – 3 of whom are of primary school age and the other four are under 4 years of age. All children are in the care of their parents – there are no orphans.

Concern about facilities and infrastructure.

Q: Will we get another doctor? Most doctors in North Clare are at capacity.
A: Please see the separate note below from the HSE about all medical services.

Q: Will we have more Gardaí and the station open?
A: The allocation of Gardaí is a matter for the Garda Commissioner.

Q: Will our health centre have additional support?
A: Please see the separate note below from the HSE about all medical services.

Q: Is their money paid through the post office and are more staff planned for the post office?
A: Yes – staffing is a matter for the local post office.

Q: What about visits from the Community and Welfare Service.?
A: The Community Welfare Service in the Department of Employment Affairs & Social Protection will attend the centre once a week to facilitate applications from residents. Staff will be administering Direct Provision Allowance (DPA) to all residents and will also be accepting and processing applications for Exceptional Need as they arise.

Q: Will our transport service be improved? There isn't much to do in Lisdoonvarna and they may wish to go further afield.
A: It is a requirement on the contractor to meet the reasonable transport need of the residents. Any additional transport needs will be organised locally to meet needs as they arise.

Appendix 1

Q: What religions will need to be accommodated? Are there facilities?
A: Applicants for international protection are not asked about their religious beliefs when they are being offered accommodation. If necessary, transport can be provided (through a local arrangement) for attendance at religious services.

Appendix 2

Follow-Up List of Questions and Answers.

Q: Has the hotel owner signed the contract with RIA?
A: As far as the department is concerned, the signing of the contracts is and was always a technicality and once our terms were agreed we were in a contractual situation with the contractor. However, for the avoidance of any doubt, the contracts have been signed.

Q: RIA in its responses claims there are four hotels operative year-round in Lisdoonvarna – there are just two – The Ritz and the Ravine.
A: There are a number of hotels in Lisdoonvarna (this is not including the hotel): Hydro Hotel, Ritz, Sheedy's Country House Hotel, Imperial Hotel and Ravine Hotel. This is not including the many hotels within close proximity to the town of Lisdoonvarna.

Q: Why is it not possible to delay opening the Direct Provision centre for 3-5 months so that the community can be consulted and adequate supports and resources put in place?
A: The number of persons seeking international protection is growing. To meet that demand and to comply with our international legal and humanitarian obligations we must ensure that we are in a position to meet the

basic needs of applicants. Our present portfolio of accommodation (34 accommodation centres all around the country) is at capacity.

Q: In addressing the question of resources, RIA responds that Lisdoon-varna has four hotels and that the conversion of the hotel to a DP centre will not affect resources. The question is not about tourist resources but about basic local services and resources (education, transport, health, and so on). RIA does not answer the key question about the pressure a centre of this size will place on already inadequate resources in Lisdoon-varna and the surrounding area.
A: Everything is being done to ensure adequate services are provided to the residents of the hotel without sacrificing the quality or availability of the services provided to those already living in the area. As per information provided to us by the Health Service Executive, GP services will be initially supplemented by a Mobile Health Screening Unit, which will provide a full medical history for review by the local GP who will ultimately provide ongoing services. No limit has been placed on the length of time that the Mobile Health Screening Unit will attend and its withdrawal will be based on clinical consultation involving the local GP and staff in the Unit.

Our colleagues in Department of Education and Skills have already been in contact with the Principal of St Enda's National School in relation to education services. As in all our other accommodation centres, the Department of Education and Tusla will work with local schools to ensure that all supports are provided.

For privacy and data protection reasons we will not make any comment on personal matters pertaining to any individual.

Q: Was a feasibility study carried out prior to arriving at the decision to open a Direct Provision centre in Lisdoonvarna?
A: Following an advertised call for expressions of interest for the provision of accommodation and ancillary services to people in the protection process a number of properties were offered to the department. All viable properties were inspected and an assessment carried out regarding

whether the proposed site was located near key services (primary school, secondary school, shop and post office).

Q: What are the criteria for locating a Direct Provision centre in a particular area?
A: That the key services outlined in question 5 are located within close proximity to the centre.

Q: What are the criteria for opening a Direct Provision centre in a particular property?
A: The provision of a high-quality accommodation centre with scope for recreation, meeting and social spaces was a key requirement in the assessment of properties offered. In addition, all interested parties were advised in the advertisement that properties being offered should largely conform with the recommendation of the Working Group on the Protection Process. This report is nearly 400 pages long and is available on the RIA web site at www.ria.gov.ie

Q: Have full health and safety checks, including fire checks, been carried out on the hotel? We would like to see the reports.
A: All relevant fire and safety checks have been made by qualified persons who are capable of assessing them. RIA has received documentation confirming this and are satisfied as to the authority and thoroughness of those who have carried out these checks.
   Like any other premises, the hotel is subject to inspection by the EHO, HSA, Data Protection Office etc.

Q: Are 'Friends of the Centre' essentially chosen from local people? Have any local groups been approached in relation to this? What financial resources are available for integration activities such volunteers/groups want to run?
A: The purpose of that group is set out in section 5.152 of the McMahon report (referred to above).

Every Direct Provision accommodation centre should be contractually obliged to encourage and facilitate linkages with the local community. The centre management should facilitate the setting up of a 'Friends of the Centre' Group consisting of residents, local statutory services and community/voluntary groups. The centre management should be required to report to RIA every six months on activities in this regard.

Work to develop community linkages should include a focus on developing reciprocal linkages with residents participating in activities in the local community and vice versa. The centre management should consider making facilities in the centre, e.g. meeting rooms and grounds, available for meetings and other activities to create and should strengthen two-way links between residents and the local community.

There are no set funds available for these groups as they are essentially operated by and for volunteers. However, the department will examine any proposal which it receives in relation to funding for specific projects.

Q: What Provision is being made for peoples' transportation needs? What official or section of what department do we contact if we have issues with their transport?
A: This contract (as is the case in all similar contracts) contains a clause requiring the contractor to meet the reasonable transport needs of the residents. Transport requirements outside of that will be provided by RIA, as necessary.

Q: Do residents have a say in what their meals are? Or when they are? If they miss a set meal will they be catered for outside of the set times? What official or section of what department do we contact if we have issues with the provision of catering provider?
A: All food is prepared and served by qualified hotel staff. Residents will be consulted about their meals to ensure that they are ethnically and

culturally appropriate. While mealtimes are generally at set times, if exten-uating circumstances mean that a resident cannot attend at those times, they can be catered for. Tea/coffee and snacks are provided 24/7.

Q: Local schools are near to full capacity. Where will children in the centre go to school?
A: Our colleagues in Department of Education and Skills have already been in contact with the Principal of St Enda's National School in relation to education services. As in all our other accommodation centres, the Department of Education and Tusla will work with local schools to ensure that all supports are provided.

For privacy and data protection reasons we will not make any comment on personal matters pertaining to any individual.

Q: Who has RIA contacted locally in relation to integration and services? What doctors, schools, and so forth has RIA been in contact with?
A: RIA is part of a multi-agency approach for the provision of services to residents of the accommodation centre. Also involved are the Health Service Executive, the Department of Education, Clare ETB and the Department of Employment Affairs and Social Protection.

Q: In relation to schools, children may have complex needs in terms of language, remedial education, trauma counselling etc. The previous correspondence mentioned three primary school-going children. What arrangements have been made with local schools about putting such provisions in place? What resources are being made available? What official or section of what department do we contact if we have issues with their education?
A: Our colleagues in Department of Education and Skills have already been in contact with the Principal of St Enda's National School in relation to education services. As in all our other accommodation centres, the Department of Education and Tusla will work with local schools to ensure that all supports are provided.

Appendix 2

For privacy and data protection reasons we will not make any comment on personal matters pertaining to any individual.

Q: What is the procedure for accessing the necessary resources – either for residents in the centre, or for local groups and services?
A: Local groups and services will continue to access resources through the channels that they have always used. Residents of the accommodation centre will be informed of what resources they are entitled to and will be provided with any necessary help (e.g. use of an interpreter where there are language difficulties).

Q: Are any of the children going to be sent to local secondary schools?
    AND
    Why weren't principals of local schools informed?
A: Our colleagues in the Department of Education and Skills have already been in contact with the Principal of St Enda's National School in relation to education services. As in all our other accommodation centres, the Department of Education and Tusla will work with local schools to ensure that all supports are provided.

For privacy and data protection reasons we will not make any comment on personal matters pertaining to any individual.

Q:Why did RIA say people were being relocated from Greece and now say something else?
A: RIA have never stated that any of the people who were being accommodated would be relocated from Greece. That programme is actually run by the Irish Refugee Protection Programme, a separate division within the Department of Justice and Equality.

Q: Does RIA know if the people coming to the centre have committed any crimes?

A: The question of crimes or criminal history of any person is a matter for the Garda Síochána. Every applicant for international protection undergoes security screening as part of that process.

Q: Is health screening compulsory for asylum seekers when they arrive?
A: Health screening is offered to all applicants for international protection and is provided during the initial reception period in Dublin.

For privacy and data protection reasons we will not make any comment on personal matters pertaining to any individual.

Q: Can RIA confirm that Stella Maris (and other specific orgs that they mention) have agreed to provide services to residents?
A: The HSE responses to earlier questions cover this point. Any necessary liaison between a doctor and Stella Maris is of course a private matter and on which we will not make any comment.

Q: Can RIA confirm that the hotel owner has been Garda-vetted?
A: It is a legal requirement that all staff working in all our centres are Garda-vetted.

Q: Are there any mechanisms in place to stop residents being exploited when volunteering?
A: Part of the function of the Friends of the Centre is to co-ordinate such volunteering and all volunteers will need to be Garda-vetted. Any suspicion of exploitation should be referred to RIA as a matter of urgency.

Q: Will RIA consult the local community in the future on the effects of the Direct Provision centre on the local economy, services, etc. and to reassess whether the centre is suitably sited?
A: RIA holds an interagency meeting with State service providers on a bi-annual basis. We will also work closely with the Friends of the Centre group. If particular issues arise, these can be brought to the attention of RIA through either of these groups.

Appendix 2

Q: In a previous meeting RIA stated that the UN would be paying for the relocation of people to Lisdoonvarna, but now it seems this is not the case. Are Irish taxpayers paying for the Direct Provision centre?
A: RIA has never stated that the UN are paying for the relocation of people to Lisdoonvarna. The costs associated with the provision of accommodation and ancillary services to people in the protection process are financed by way of general exchequer funding.

Q: Is there anything to stop the hotel owner tendering for another centre in the area? Can we get an assurance from RIA that this won't happen?
A: The public procurement process is open to any party (or indeed a group of persons/communities) who meets the qualification criteria specified in a request for tender document. However, it should be noted that it is not the intention of RIA to run a public procurement process for another accommodation centre in Lisdoonvarna during the lifetime of this contract.

Q: Can we get an age breakdown of the children who are arriving?
A: For privacy and data protection reasons we will not make any comment on personal matters pertaining to any individual.

Q: Can RIA provide a timeline of when people are arriving and what needs to be in place so that people can prepare.
A: The first phase involves approximately 30 people and it is intended that they will arrive at the hotel during the week 12/03/2018 - 18/03/2018.

Q: Can we have nominated liaisons from the community who Justice/RIA can work with and who can raise community concerns with RIA?
A: This is managed through the Friends of the Centre group – see the more detailed response above.

Q: Is the hotel owner going to be running the Direct Provision centre, and what are his credentials for taking care of people who are seeking asylum?

Appendix 2

A: The contract is between the department and the hotel to provide hotel-type services to residents. The Reception and Integration Agency must be informed of all staff who will be working in the centre. Through the existing inspection service, RIA will be working closely with staff to ensure that a quality service is provided to all residents at all times. Arrangements have already been made to provide staff with additional diversity and cultural awareness training. All children in the centre are in the care of their parents.

Q: Will people working in the centre be Garda-vetted?
A: All persons working with those in the protection process are required to undergo Garda vetting and also to receive training relevant to their particular role.

Q: Has anyone considered if there is a legal onus on the government to carry out an impact study before imposing a centre of this size on a small community?
A: Following an advertised call for expressions of interest for the provision of accommodation and ancillary services to people in the protection process a number of properties were offered to the department. All viable properties were inspected and an assessment carried out regarding whether the proposed site was located near key services (primary school, secondary school, shop and post office).

Q: What precautions, procedures, training and safety measures are being put in place to ensure that the safety and welfare of children in the centre will be safeguarded? What official or section of what department do we contact if we have issues with child safety at the facility?
A: Staff working in accommodation centres are required to undergo child safety training and to be Garda-vetted. RIA have a child protection and welfare policy and staff from RIA's Child and Family Services Unit will be working closely with staff from the centre to ensure best practice in relation to child welfare issues. RIA's child protection and welfare policy can be

accessed at the RIA website. All children in the centre are in the care of their parents.

Q: RIA and White have mentioned staff in the hotel being trained and vetted but to our knowledge there have been no staff in situ since October – so how is this possible?
A: The matter of staffing is a question for the contractor themselves. RIA, however, have been given the details of all those working in the centre. All members of staff will require Garda vetting and any other relevant vetting or training that befits their role. Please see our answer to question 30 above in relation to the provision of training and upskilling of staff.

Q: Is RIA aware that Tusla does not have a child protection welfare officer in Clare? When will Clare be appointed a child protection welfare officer?
A: RIA provides the training in Child Protection Procedures and its own Child Protection Policy through the Child and Family Unit, which is managed by a seconded Tusla Social Work Team Leader. If child protection concerns arise for any child, the Centre's Designated Liaison Person and the Child and Family Support Unit manager liaise with the Local Social Work Team and make appropriate referrals to that service.

Q: RIA alleges that the Mobile Health Unit, along with community welfare officers and other essential supports, will be available to the residents on a weekly basis. Is RIA's statement a guarantee that if these do not materialise, that residents have a legal right to be provided with all of the services RIA outline in their responses? What official or section of what department do we contact if we have issues with their healthcare?
A: Under the Direct Provision system health services are provided and coordinated by the HSE. As to the question of who to contact regarding issues for healthcare, as always these would be matters for the HSE. Please see their detailed answers provided in an earlier response.

Appendix 2

Q: RIA alleges that the contractor is obliged to provide and pay for the necessary transportation for residents. If this does not materialise, do residents have a legal right to demand such vital transport services?

A: It is a contractual obligation that the reasonable transport needs of the residents are met by the contractor. Additional transport needs will be met by RIA.